T0079688

WINE

Edible

Series Editor: Andrew F. Smith

EDIBLE is a revolutionary new series of books dedicated to food and drink that explores the rich history of cuisine. Each book reveals the global history and culture of one type of food or beverage.

Already published

Apple Erika Janik *Beef* Lorna Piatti-Farnell *Bread* William Rubel *Cake* Nicola Humble *Caviar* Nichola Fletcher *Champagne* Becky Sue Epstein *Cheese* Andrew Dalby *Chocolate* Sarah Moss and Alexander Badenoch *Cocktails* Joseph M. Carlin *Curry* Colleen Taylor Sen *Dates* Nawal Nasrallah *Gin* Lesley Jacobs Solmonson *Hamburger* Andrew F. Smith *Herbs* Gary Allen *Hot Dog* Bruce Kraig *Ice Cream* Laura B. Weiss *Lemon* Toby Sonneman *Lobster* Elisabeth Townsend *Milk* Hannah Velten *Offal* Nina Edwards *Olive* Fabrizia Lanza *Oranges* Clarissa Hyman *Pancake* Ken Albala *Pie* Janet Clarkson *Pizza* Carol Helstosky *Pork* Katharine M. Rogers *Potato* Andrew F. Smith *Rum* Richard Foss *Sandwich* Bee Wilson *Soup* Janet Clarkson *Spices* Fred Czarra *Tea* Helen Saberi *Whiskey* Kevin R. Kosar *Wine* Marc Millon

Wine

A Global History

Marc Millon

REAKTION BOOKS

For Kim, my companion in wine and in life

Published by Reaktion Books Ltd
33 Great Sutton Street
London EC1V 0DX, UK
www.reaktionbooks.co.uk

First published 2013

Printed and bound in China by C&C Offset Printing Co., Ltd

British Library Cataloguing in Publication Data
Millon, Marc.
Wine: a global history. – (Edible)
1. Wine and wine making – History.
I. Title II. Series
641.2´2´09-DC23

ISBN 978 1 78023 111 2

Contents

Introduction

Wine is the most wondrous, complex, mysterious and magical of all man's agricultural creations. At the same time, it is one of the simplest and most natural.

At its most basic, wine is simply the fermented juice of fresh grapes. *Vitis vinifera* wine grapes contain a high concentration of fructose. Once crushed, natural yeasts present on the skin of the grapes feed on this sugar, converting it to alcohol and giving off carbon dioxide as a by-product. The result is a fermented beverage that may or may not be potable. If left exposed to air, it will quickly spoil and turn to undrinkable vinegar. But nurture it carefully and it can be conserved for months, years, decades – even centuries.

The origins of wine go back to the origins of modern humankind. As early man emerged from a nomadic hunter-gatherer way of life and began to embark on one of settled domestication, it would seem that the practice of gathering grapes for the making of a fermented beverage, wine, developed – perhaps as early as 8,000 years ago. From its earliest origins, most probably in the Transcaucasus, the grape vine quickly spread across Asia Minor and the Mediterranean, and wine became something of a symbol of civilization itself.

Indeed, almost from the earliest days of its discovery and creation, wine was considered something special, almost divine. No doubt the considerable effort necessary to produce wine meant that it was perforce the most highly valued and precious of agricultural products. Consider what went into – what still goes into – the creation of wine: the careful nurturing and cultivation of the plant for a period of years before it is able to bear fruit; the annual cycle of work in the vineyard leading to a single, once-a-year harvest; the careful collection of the grapes and their transport to a winemaking facility; the pressing of the grapes and the alcoholic fermentation to transform juice into wine; and the storage of the finished wine itself in a way that ensures it does not spoil. Add to this the fact that wine has the ability to induce altered states of consciousness and it is not hard to see why from its earliest origins it was so highly prized, becoming imbued with connotations of the divine and miraculous.

Indeed, from those earliest days, wine was considered a drink for kings and nobles. Across civilizations, from the Sumerians to the Egyptians, wine was not only enjoyed at the most important moments in the here-and-now, but even accompanied personages of the highest birth on their journeys to the afterlife.

Wine, a drink for kings, pharoahs and warriors, was considered a veritable gift from the gods. Cults based around the consumption and enjoyment of wine sprang up in ancient Greece and Rome, while wine became a central element in both Hebrew and Christian ritual and liturgy. The daily requirement for wine to celebrate the miracle of the Eucharist – the transubstantiation of wine into the blood of Christ – meant that as Christianity spread to the New World and beyond, vineyards needed to be planted for the production of wine for the quotidian celebration of Mass.

Amphora, probably made in Cyprus, 300–100 BC. The amphora was
the vessel of transport and storage for wine in the ancient world.
Amphorae could be stacked in the holds of ships for transport across
the Mediterranean and were easily handled due to their shape and size.

Today grape vines are planted all around the globe. Wine is now not only a beverage for marking significant moments in religious and secular life, but it is also an essential daily staple for many. Indeed, the regular consumption and enjoyment of wine with meals is part of the European lifestyle and culture that has immense global appeal. Wine consumption is on the increase in countries such as the United Kingdom and the United States, as well as in emerging wine-drinking countries across India, Southeast Asia and the Far East.

How did *Vitis vinifera*, a single species from the genus *Vitis* probably originating in the Transcaucasus, spread so successfully all around the world? Today the grape vine is found on every continent on earth with the exception of Antarctica. And why grapes? After all, virtually all fruits and many other parts of plants are fermentable, able to have their natural sugars converted into an alcoholic beverage: witness cider from apples; fruit wines; rice wine; various distillations made from grain, potatoes and other carbohydrates; and beer from malted barley. Yet wine produced from fresh grapes is unique. Not only is it able to produce a magnificent alcoholic libation, but it is also the only such beverage that has an entire culture and even a cult surrounding its production and consumption.

The story of wine is an utterly compelling one. This volume only scratches the surface as it delves into the story within your glass. It is my hope that it will spark your interest and lead to more in-depth exploration. For to gain an understanding of where wine comes from, its history and traditions, its infinite variety, and the culture of wine and wine drinking, is to gain a richer understanding and enjoyment of this, the most wondrous, complex and fascinating beverage on earth.

I

The Wine Grape

> And Noah began to be a husbandman, and he planted
> a vineyard: and he drank of the wine, and was drunken;
> and he was uncovered within his tent (Genesis 9:20–21)

Noah was most definitely not the first human to enjoy – and to suffer – the intoxicating effects of that most magical, noble and wondrous of all beverages, wine. Archaeological evidence indicates that our Neolithic ancestors, somewhere in Asia Minor, began to cultivate the domesticated grapevine, *Vitis vinifera*, possibly as long ago as 6000 BC.

This tenacious Eurasian creeper grew prolifically in its wild manifestation in the temperate climate across the Transcaucasus, Anatolia, Turkey and the Middle East, and possibly over Mediterranean lands, too. Originally prehistoric hunter-gatherers would simply have collected the wild berries, along with anything else edible. It is not hard to imagine a surplus of wild grapes fermenting of its own accord due to the action of wild yeasts present on the grape skins feeding on the fruit's own natural sugars. The haphazard result, if less palatable than today's precisely controlled vintages, would nonetheless have had a similarly exhilarating and mind-altering effect: intoxication.

Imagine, in a world in which life was undoubtedly 'nasty, brutish and short', what a divine potation this rudimentary wine must have been, an elixir that had the power to transport early man from out of his own ugly and brutal existence to a land beyond dreams. No wonder that, from the earliest ages, wine has been considered a gift of the gods.

The domestication of plants and animals allowed Neolithic man to build communities that could be lived in as permanent settlements all year round – the origins of Western civilization as we know it. Is it mere coincidence that the cradles of civilization are in those temperate areas where

Wine storage jar decorated with mountain goats, Iran, 4th millenium BC.

The movement of quantities of liquid – whether wine or oil – presented our ancestors with technological challenges. This terracotta model unearthed in Cyprus and dating from 600–500 BC illustrates a two-wheeled cart on which is perched a biconical amphora, allowing wine to be moved, whether from cellar to private dwelling or even longer distances.

V. vinifera was able to thrive? The development of systematic agriculture resulted in a more secure and ample supply of foodstuffs than did haphazard nomadic gathering, and more permanent settlements and homes allowed for the development of ever more sophisticated means of consumption, including cooking, baking and the mastering of fermentation for the making of bread, beer and wine.

The development of pottery would seem to have been central to the development of systematic winemaking, for liquid fermentation required vessels large enough to hold quantities of grape juice. Smaller vessels allowed for the storage of the resulting wine. Pottery vessels began to appear around 6000 BC and scientific analysis has confirmed the presence of wine in clay pots found in the mountains of northern Iran, dating back to around 5000 BC.

Once wine could be stored, perhaps in pots buried in the earth to keep it cool or set aside in the constant temperature of caves, it could be conserved for a period of months or even longer without spoiling. Thus it did not need to be consumed immediately but could be reserved for the most important banquets, rituals and social, civic and religious occasions, as well as for possible everyday consumption, though probably only by the top echelon of society.

Vitis vinifera

The grapevine belongs to the botanical family Ampelidaceae, which includes any number of vigorous, climbing plants. There are literally thousands of vine species, with those suitable for grape-bearing all belonging to the genus *Vitis*. Of the numerous *Vitis* species, *V. vinifera*, native to Europe, Asia and the Near East, has emerged overwhelmingly as the most important for winemaking. Other varieties include *V. labrusca*, native to North America, and *V. amurensis* from the Far East, as well as *V. riparia*, *V. rupestris* and *V. berlandieri*, among others.

What is so special about *V. vinifera*? Quite simply, *V. vinifera* grapes, grown under the right conditions, have the capacity to fully concentrate natural sugars up to one-third of their weight in volume. This, combined with a natural balance of acidity, plus tannin and other constituent elements and flavour compounds, allowed for the production of wines that could be conserved. In other words, *V. vinifera* had the greatest potential and capacity to produce wines with sufficient alcohol and other elements that would enable them to remain drinkable, rather than to deteriorate quickly and spoil into unpalatable vinegar or worse.

V. v. silvestris, the wild grapevine, produced fruit that was enjoyed haphazardly by our hunter-gatherer ancestors. In those areas where they still grow, wild grapevines remain a mixture

Nebbiolo grapes growing in the Barolo vineyards of Italy's Piedmont.
The majority of the world's wine, today as in the ancient past, is produced
from *V. vinifera*, a species of the grapevine native to Europe, Asia and the
Near East.

of both male and female plants. Over the course of probably centuries, if not millennia, through early man's selection, the cultivated variety, *V. v. sativa*, came to be a fruitful hermaphrodite plant that is able to self-propagate. Ever since, the evolution of the grapevine has been one of ever-increasing selection and adaptation. Indeed, one of the great features of *V. vinifera* is its tenacious ability to adapt to different environments and microclimates, even mutating where necessary in order to survive.

Man has continually assisted in this process by selecting those grapes that thrive best in each specific vineyard environment. It is no mere coincidence that particular grape varieties have been planted in and grow particularly well in specific soils, terrains and climates, and not in others.

Strength in Biodiversity

Today there are literally hundreds, if not thousands, of varieties of *V. vinifera* vines producing wine grapes that have adapted to unique vineyard conditions all around the wine-growing world. Each variety has its own quintessential flavour and character, though this can differ considerably when the same variety is grown under different conditions, whether on the other side of the world, or even in adjoining vineyards of differing terrain within the same region, sub-region or community.

Today *V. vinifera* grapevines grow in high mountain slopes in the Alps in Italy's Valle d'Aosta, and almost buried in deep, windblown sandpits at Portugal's Colares; in the high rarefied atmosphere of the Andes in Chile and Argentina, and across the hellishly hot steppes of central Russia; in vineyards planted by missionaries in California and by settlers who brought the vine with them to grow in South Africa's Cape; across the wide continent of Australia, and over the cool-climate sites of New Zealand's South Island. Wines are made from grapes grown across the United States even in places like Texas, North Carolina, Virginia, Idaho and Ohio; and increasing numbers of wines – good wines – are produced from grapes grown throughout England and Wales. Meanwhile, in the Far East, China is emerging as one of the fastest-growing new wine-producing countries as land is given over to the planting of *V. vinifera* to satisfy a growing thirst for European-style wines from the world's largest and most populous country. Already, surprisingly, China is among the top ten wine-producing countries in the world.

Some grape varieties seem only to grow in very specific areas, on certain terrains or in special microclimates. Others, it seems, are able to be transplanted and adapt to conditions that vary considerably, all over the world. Witness the great success of internationally prolific grapes such as cabernet sauvignon, merlot, chardonnay and sauvignon blanc at adapting to the most diverse conditions, terrains and microclimates.

If the vine's natural propensity to adapt to new conditions is one enduring feature of this fascinating plant, another is that through the intervention of man new varieties can be created from old by crossing varieties together. The popular German grape müller-thurgau was created from a cross of riesling and silvaner more than a hundred years ago, resulting in a new variety that is fairly prolific as well as being easier to cultivate than the temperamental riesling. There are many more grape varieties that have been similarly created through the ingenuity of man.

Furthermore, research into the best clones of the same grape varieties continues apace. Clonal selection allows the winegrower to choose examples of vines with particular attributes or characteristics. One clone might fare better in a particular soil; another might be more resistant to viral disease; while yet another might produce wines with slightly higher or lower acidity, depending on a winegrower's particular requirements. In the 'Chianti Classico 2000' research project, more than 200 clones of the main grape types used to make chianti classico were analysed, from which 24 preferred clones of the grape sangiovese were selected, each with particular and individual attributes.

Hybrid Grapes

V. vinifera may produce the vast majority of the world's wines – and certainly the best – but wines from grapes from other species are also produced. Most notably, the *V. labrusca* vine proliferates across North America and the grapes it yields have long been used to make distinctive (if sometimes repellent to those with European tastes) wines in states such as Ohio and New York. These were possibly the vines discovered by the Norseman Leif Ericson, who is credited as being the first European to set foot in the Americas in the year 1003, leaving a settlement behind in a land that he named Vinland, possibly in what is present-day New England. There is no evidence that Leif and his fellow Norsemen made or enjoyed wine from the grapes they found, but the vine must have been a dominant feature for the new land to have been so named.

Today hybrid grapes have been developed that are crosses from different species, *V. vinifera* with *V. labrusca* or *V. amurensis*. These hybrid grapes, though prohibited or shunned in the established vineyards of Europe, nevertheless are capable of producing noteworthy wines in those areas where the successful cultivation of *V. vinifera* is marginal at best, such

Seyval grapes growing in Devon, England. Hybrid grape varieties, which are crosses of *V. vinifera* with other species such as *V. labrusca*, may be capable of producing noteworthy wines in those areas where the successful cultivation of grapes from pure *V. vinifera* is marginal at best.

as in England and parts of North America. Indeed, in Britain, in recent years and decades, an increasing number of vineyards have been planted primarily with hybrid grapes such as seyval, madeleine angevin, rondo and others, and the results have been encouraging.

Phylloxera vastatrix

By the middle of the nineteenth century, the great and minor vineyards of Europe were all mainly well established, with deep roots that extended in some cases back to the days of the ancient Romans, Greeks and beyond. Imagine, then, the horror when a voracious aphid that came to be christened *Phylloxera vastatrix* – 'the devastator' – was discovered in France when it began eating its way through the roots of vineyards across the country, killing the plants in the process. Few vineyard areas were to escape its ravages, save those whose roots lay in near pure sand, as in parts of the French Languedoc. All the rest were destroyed, one by one, a catastrophe that devastated the economies and livelihoods of winegrowers throughout France. Vineyards were fumigated in an attempt to eradicate the pest, but ultimately most succumbed, in many cases never to be replanted. *P. vastatrix* was not only voracious, but also fast-moving, and eventually spread across the vineyards of Europe by the 1920s.

After much soul searching and experimentation, eventually a radical solution was found. The pest, it seemed, could not have originated in Europe, or else the vines would have developed some sort of natural defence to combat it. If *P. vastatrix* came from America, whose vines were apparently immune to it, what would happen if European vines were grafted on to *Phylloxera*-resistant American rootstock? Though in some quarters there was great resistance to this solution, in the end it was accepted that *Phylloxera* could not be fully eradicated by chemical means, and there was no alternative but for vineyards to be completely grubbed up and then replanted with *Vitis vinifera* grafted on rootstock from varieties such as *V. labrusca*.

Thus the virtual wholesale replantation of Europe's main vineyards took place over the course of the early decades of the twentieth century. Though at the time some connoisseurs considered the resulting post-*Phylloxera* wines to be inferior to those produced pre-*Phylloxera*, this solution had been the only way to save the entire European wine industry.

The need to replant Europe's vineyards led to the abandonment of areas where winegrowing was marginal at best (and the wines mainly indifferent), while in the classic wine regions, the concept of systematic grape growing under legally defined restraints led to the creation of the *appellation d'origine contrôlée* (AOC) in France. The AOC defined such important matters as permitted grape varieties, yields, winemaking processes and ageing disciplines, and served to give consumers something of a guarantee as to the authenticity and origin of a wine so that they could identify and enjoy wines with greater confidence.

The Concept of *Terroir*

Critical to the French approach is *terroir*, a term for which there is no precise English translation. *Terroir* indicates the combination of characteristics – geographical, climatic and microclimatic, as well as historic and human – that go into the making of a wine. At its heart is the belief that the better the wine, the more precisely its origin can be pinpointed, for it is only wines with immense and particular personalities that are able to demonstrate the uniqueness of their individual and particularly precise *terroirs*.

The region of Burgundy, for example, produces pinot noir wines that are different from pinot noir wines produced anywhere elsewhere in the world. Those from Burgundy's Côte d'Or may have deeper and more profound flavours and personality than those entitled only to the simple regional burgundy appellation. A specific village or communal appellation, such as gevrey-chambertin or vosne-romanée, is more precise still, with wines displaying characteristics unique to their places of origin. Finally, the greatest and most individual wines come from individually classified vineyards that have been granted their own particular appellations, as in le chambertin or la romanée. Such wines are the pinnacle, the highest and greatest expression of *terroir*, and may be granted further classified accolades such as premier or grand cru status.

The Gallic reasoning, quite simply and logically, is that quality in wine is defined by the unique circumstances of a wine's *terroir*. Those wines that are capable of expressing the most distinct personality and individuality can be identified by ever more precise appellations, even down to individual plots of land.

The concept of *terroir* as defined and systematically catalogued by AOC is not confined only to France, but has been similarly applied throughout the classic wine regions of Europe, with *denominazione d'origine controllata* (DOC) in Italy and *denominación de origen* (DO) in Spain both to some extent mirroring the French model of AOC. In Germany, the quality classifications *Qualitätswein bestimmter Anbaugebiete* (QbA) and *Qualitätswein mit Prädikat* (QmP) both identify wines by place of origin, in some cases individual vineyard, as well as by grape variety and, for QmP wines, by levels of ripeness.

The French concept of *terroir* is based on the premise that wine is a unique product that is the result of the totality of myriad elements that go into its creation – geographical, climatic and microclimatic, as well as cultural and human.

The Varietal Approach

To European sensibilities, *terroir* has thus long served to define the wines we drink and enjoy – St Emilion, Alsace, Barolo, Rioja and Rheingau are all at once names of both wines and towns or regions of origin. This is fundamental to an understanding and appreciation of wines from the classic regions of Europe.

And yet, is place really more important to the wine drinker than the most fundamental element that goes into the creation of a wine: the grape, *V. vinifera*? Throughout the New World, as well as increasingly in Europe, wines are identified and marketed primarily by the principal grape variety used to produce them. Drinkers may choose a chardonnay, sauvignon blanc, merlot, pinot grigio, cabernet sauvignon or pinot noir, for example. Place of origin is still important, of course, but increasingly it is the name of the producer, or more likely the brand, that consumers come to seek and trust.

It is easy to see why today's generation of wine drinkers may prefer such an approach. The knowledge required to be able to discern the different nuances between village appellations or to make sense of the confusing number of Italian regional and local wine *denominazioni* based on sometimes obscure geographical names is not easily acquired. It is of course far simpler to select by grape variety and by brand. But to do so solely, without reference to place and *terroir*, is to miss out on a tier of understanding and appreciation that can add considerably to the enjoyment of a glass or bottle of wine.

A World of Flavours

Paradoxically, it would seem that the varietal approach, rather than leading to a greater understanding and appreciation of the grapes from which wine is made, may be having the opposite effect. For indeed, rather than celebrating the immense biodiversity of *V. vinifera* and the myriad grape varieties from which wines are made, are we not, in fact, seeing an ever decreasing number of grape varieties used to produce the wines that most people drink? The rise and rise of global brands means that, increasingly and sadly, the wealth of indigenous, local grapes with names known to few is being replaced by a mere handful of so-called international varieties known and recognized by their safe, familiar names and flavours.

Our ancestors mastered the cultivation of *V. vinifera* thousands of years ago, and down the ages, man's ingenuity has led to the development and creation of the most complex and wonderful beverage on earth – wine. The number of grape varieties still grown and the variety of wines produced around the world remains immense, the styles and types of wine remarkably and ingeniously diverse. The tenacious ability of the vine to adapt to different global environments and circumstances ensured its survival. Let us hope that the tenacious thirst and curiosity of today's and tomorrow's adventurous wine drinkers will ensure the enduring survival of wine in all its glorious variety and biodiversity.

2
Across Wine-dark Seas: A Brief Overview of the Spread of Viticulture

Vitis vinifera has proved itself a tenacious plant, able to survive and thrive in diverse regions, countries and continents that display extreme variations in climate and micro-climate. It is fascinating to consider how viticulture has spread around the world.

Early Origins

Where did wine begin? Patrick McGovern, a leading expert on the origins of ancient wine, was involved in the discovery of what is possibly Neolithic man's earliest known identifiable wine in Hajji Firuz Tepe, an archaeological site in the Zagros Mountains of Iran. Here McGovern and his colleagues discovered the remains of clay vessels that contained the residue of what scientific analysis has indicated to be the fermented juice of grapes: wine. The site dates from *c.* 5400–5000 BC and is significant as it is considered the earliest evidence of wine-making on a domestic scale.

While historical and ancient texts may be based on legend and hearsay, McGovern's research has demonstrated that archaeology and other natural sciences can provide concrete evidence of the earliest attempts at the systematic production of wine.

Clay fragments containing, for example, the residues of tartaric acid and calcium tartrate are evidence of wine, for only wine can be expected to contain these substances in quantities sufficient to be measured. Yeast residues are further evidence of fermentation. The presence of tree residues indicates that such primitive wines were often resinated, perhaps as a preservative.

By comparing the DNA from the wild grape *V. vinifera silvestris* to that of modern cultivars, McGovern and his colleagues hope to be able to go even further: to pinpoint the precise transition from haphazard winemaking from wild grapes to the systematic production of wine from the domesticated *V. v. sativa*.

How the fermented juice of grapes was first unintentionally obtained is not difficult to imagine. Stone Age man, foraging in some fertile river valley, perhaps in the upland regions of what are now Georgia, Turkey, Armenia, Azerbaijan or Iran, would have encountered wild vines laden with a berry-like fruit: grapes. Who could resist picking and tasting them: at once sweet and tart? The grapes would have been gathered to eat just so, and any surplus would have been placed perhaps in an animal hide, in a stone trough or receptacle, or in a wooden hollow. The weight from the topmost grapes would crush those below, the bloom of yeast on the skin would set off a natural fermentation feeding on the grape sugars, and the resultant liquid would be a wine of sorts, low in alcohol, yet a fermented beverage all the same. It would have had to be consumed quickly before it spoiled, and consumption in quantity and haste would have only emphasized its mind-altering effects.

If such a result could come from serendipidity, the potential to create such wondrous nectar regularly would have presented prehistoric man with a considerable challenge and opportunity. The uniquely human condition, from the earliest mists of time, has been to use our intelligence, ingenuity and innate mental skills to find solutions to problems inherent not just in the survival of the species, but in the creation and development of civilization itself.

Consider, then, some of the steps needed to progress from incidental fruit gathering and accidental fermentation, to domesticated viticulture and systematic viniculture. A concerted effort over generations, across centuries, would have been required to transform the wild grape vine *V. v. sylvestris* into its cultivated relative *V. v. sativa* through the selection of self-propagating plants that not only fertilized more consistently but also yielded superior fruit. Vineyards would have needed to be cared for throughout the year, a substantial undertaking, considering that newly planted vines would not

Beauty and function are inextricably linked, as in this pair of wine vessels dating from 2700 BC, possibly used for mixing wine with water or other flavourings, as was often done in the ancient world.

The story of wine is revealed on myriad artefacts unearthed from the ancient world. This marble Roman sarcophagus, for example, illustrates the reduction of *mustum* – freshly pressed grape juice – by boiling in a cauldron. The *mustum* may have been used to sweeten wines.

yield fruit for the first few years and that the bounty of the plant results in but a single harvest per year.

Once the grapes were carefully harvested, the skills relating to systematic winemaking even at the most basic level would have been not inconsiderable. If *V. vinifera* grapes, when fully ripe, could be carefully cultivated to achieve sufficient sugar levels to result in a fermented wine in excess of, say at least eight or nine degrees alcohol per volume (any less than this would have resulted in an unstable product), further steps would have been needed to achieve more consistent and satisfactory results. Early man realized that oxygen was a spoiler, turning wine to vinegar, so steps were taken to reduce its effects. For example, once the production of clay pottery was mastered, squat clay vessels with pot bellies and narrow necks were produced that could be sealed with clay or with wooden stoppers to keep out air. In other cases, the ancients added aromatic resins to wine, both to serve as a preservative and to mask any unpleasant flavours.

The process of systematic viticulture and winemaking has roots that extend back into the deepest mists of time and research into the origins of wine continues. But what is certain is that no other agricultural product required anywhere near as much care in cultivation and in subsequent time-consuming processing before it could be enjoyed. Wine alone was – *is* – unique. The results of such considerable efforts were prized and valued indeed: the creation of a special and unique beverage that was almost considered divine!

A Drink for Kings, Queens and Pharoahs

From the earliest ages, this most special of beverages enjoyed something of a sacred and certainly a royal reputation. Surely only the most exalted and privileged could afford the luxury of something requiring such care and time to produce. It is no surprise that such an exalted beverage was treated with the utmost reverence and respect and, from the earliest ages, a culture of wine and wine drinking evolved.

Silver-covered vineshoots dating back to 3000 BC have been discovered in burial mounds in southern Georgia – perhaps, who knows, to enable the deceased to carry the vine with them into some imagined fertile afterlife (indeed, who can imagine paradise without wine?). Assyrian bas-reliefs illustrate kings enjoying cups of wine under shaded bowers of grapes. The Sumerian Hammurabi's Code has strictures relating to wine shops, and artefacts from Queen Puabi's burial chamber include fluted gold wine cups and goblets. Wine was a feature of life throughout Anatolia and a sophisticated wine culture was evident in the elaborate drinking vessels, jugs and storage vessels used in royal celebrations. Beautiful Hittite silver drinking horns in the shape of animals have been discovered dating from 1600 BC.

Though the wild grape was probably not native to Egypt, there was a thriving wine industry there as early as the beginning of the Old Kingdom (around 3000 BC). We can thus learn

Fragment of a basalt clepsydra (water clock) depicting Philip Arrhidaeus wearing the red crown, and projecting kilt with bull's tail, and offering two jars of wine. Egypt, *c.* 320 BC.

Wine has always been considered a libation for kings, warriors and a ruling elite. This Assyrian gypsum wall panel, unearthed in northern Iraq, shows an enthroned queen and reclining king feasting in an arbour amid vines, an image of earthly paradise.

Egyptian wine jar, 18th or 19th Dynasty. Jars such as these contained vintage wines, placed in tombs to provide sustenance in the next world. This jar is dedicated to the Lady Nedjnet (1340–1300 BC).

about ancient winemaking processes from Egyptian tomb paintings that depict grape-laden, trellised vineyards as well as detailed images of winemaking, from the treading of grapes barefoot to the storage of wine in a variety of earthenware jars. There are depictions, too, of the enjoyment of wine, drinking from wine cups by royal personages and scenes of joyous feasting. Wine, it seems, from the earliest ages has been associated with feasting and celebration at the highest level.

In the pharoahs' tombs, there were 'wine cellars' filled with wine jars to accompany them on their journeys into an eternal and happy afterlife. When Tutankhamun's tomb was unearthed, among the many splendid and wondrous treasures discovered

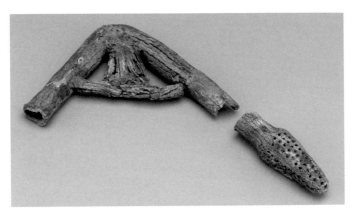

The culture of wine drinking in ancient Egypt was well developed and pharaohs' tombs were lined with wine cellars to accompany them on their journey to an afterlife. Numerous wine-related artefacts have been unearthed, such as this perforated drinking tube or wine strainer dating from the 18th Dynasty.

were 26 amphorae of wine. Some fifteen winemakers are recorded by name on the wine-jar labels. The provenance and age of vintages was also noted, with wine jars designated as coming from different estates and even from Syria, and of varying ages. It seems that older wines, in antiquity as today, were considered the most valuable, for surely only the best, the greatest wines, would have been entombed to slake the thirst of a pharaoh on his final, and who knows how long, journey.

The Spread of Viticulture

The vine is a tenacious plant and one that is easy to transplant: stick a cutting in the ground and a plant will take root. The grape vine, it appears, quickly spread from its original source in the Transcaucasus, Asia Minor and Mesopotamia across the Levant to Mediterranean lands. It seems the Mediterranean climatic conditions, as well as the varied terrains, were ideally suited to the cultivation of *V. vinifera*, with diurnal temperatures and rhythms providing sufficient heat by day to allow for the ripening of grapes during the growing season, and the freshness by night required to maintain a balance of fruity acidity that helped to preserve the resulting wines. Average precipitation provided sufficient moisture to allow the grapes to swell.

Certainly the grape vine was well established across the Middle East. During the second millennium BC, Phoenician traders, mainly from Tyre and Sidon in modern Lebanon, carried the vine with them on journeys that took them across North Africa and the Italian peninsula, and eventually to Iberia. Present-day Cádiz, in Andalusia, was one such Phoenician trading outpost, and it is probable that the vineyards that now produce sherry, one of the great wines of the world, were originally planted by these intrepid seafarers.

Recent archaeological discoveries in the fabled ancient city of Petra, in what is now Jordan, have revealed beautiful ancient wall paintings that demonstrate the importance of wine to the Nabataeans. Though the Nabataeans were originally nomads, they eventually settled and created a trading network across the Middle East that was annexed into the Roman Empire. Recent evidence indicates that Petra was surrounded by ancient vineyards and grape-pressing sites, subjects depicted in the newly found wall paintings.

Earlier still, the Greek mainland and islands of the Aegean had been settled by peoples who delighted in the cultivation of the vine and the olive, two plants that have come to symbolize Western civilization. Both yielded liquid products that could be easily transported, and this contributed to the development of sea trade and the consequent exchange of ideas as well as social mobility through the spread of colonies. Indeed, the vine was soon being cultivated across what is now mainland Greece, as well as on islands throughout the Aegean, on Greek outposts on the Italian and Iberian peninsulas, and across to the Black Sea. Individual islands became known for their wines, notably Chios and Lesbos, both located in the Eastern Mediterranean. Such wines, transported in identifiable amphorae – double-handled clay vases holding up to 40 litres – unique to each place, were the basis of economic trade in the ancient world.

In this era, much of southern Italy and Sicily was known as Magna Graecia, and grape varieties still cultivated today indicate Hellenic roots, such as aglianico and greco. Such vines from Greco-Italian vineyards were prized in antiquity. A tiny, now forgotten wine outpost in Calabria known as Cirò was once the famous source of Kremissa wine, traditionally the libation for victorious athletes in the ancient Hellenic Olympic games.

Across the lands and islands settled by the various Greek factions, countless archaeological artefacts and ruins have been unearthed that demonstrate the central place of wine to the ancients: amphorae for the transportation of wine; beautifully decorated wine cups and mixing bowls; and friezes depicting vines and wine, and the drinking and enjoyment of wine by man and god alike.

That wine – good, deeply coloured wine – had become a feature of Grecian life is evident in the blind poet Homer's references to the 'wine-dark seas' and the depiction of wine drinking as both quotidian activity and sacred ritual. Wine features throughout both the *Iliad* and the *Odyssey*. Libations are continually offered to the gods, and the men drink freely by the ships beached at Troy, while the warrior Achilles sulks in his tent. Wine is always offered to guests as a mark of hospitality, and summits take place over the sharing of wine.

What was wine like in ancient times? From E. V. Rieu's translation of Homer's *Odyssey*, we gain a glimpse:

> I took with me in a goatskin some dark and mellow wine that had been given to me by Maron son of Euanthes . . . This man had given me some fine presents: seven talents of wrought gold, with a mixing-bowl of solid silver, and he drew off for me a dozen jars of mellow unmixed wine as well. It was a wonderful drink. It had been kept secret from all his serving-men and maids, in fact from everyone in the house but himself, his good wife and a housekeeper. To drink this red and honeyed vintage, he would pour one cupful of wine into twenty of water, and the bouquet that rose from the bowl was pure heaven – those were occasions when abstinence could have no charms.

What an epic wine Maron's must have been! And certainly, though we would rarely consider diluting with such a quantity of water, we can well imagine the heavenly bouquet of such a magnificent vintage.

Wine helped to heal the body as well as the mind. Hippocrates, the father of medicine, considered that wine could heal any number of ailments, prescribing particular wines to cure a variety of conditions and even stipulating the temperatures at which they were to be taken. Warm wine was mixed with aromatic spices and honey, a concoction that does not sound that different from the sort of mulled wine or hot toddy that we might drink to pick us up when we're feeling poorly or under the weather.

The ancient Greeks rarely drank their wines unmixed. Indeed, the ritual of mixing wine was an important one, and the skills required to achieve desirable potations were highly valued in Greek society. Wines were mixed with water or

Greek temple at Metaponto, Basilicata. The spread of viticulture across
the Mediterranean was in large part due to the efforts of the Greeks. Much
of the southern Italian peninsula formed part of Magna Graecia and
grape varieties still cultivated today can be traced back to Hellenic origins.

Red gigure calyx krater depicting Nike pouring an offering of wine into a dish held by Poseidon, *c.* 480–460 BC.

seawater, and they sometimes had aromatics, spices, herbs or honey added to them. Such libations would be enjoyed at male gatherings: the word 'symposium' refers simply to drinking together. The symposium became an important social gathering where men gathered to discuss the most pressing issues of the day, or to discourse on subjects such as poetry, philosophy, medicine, music or love. The drinking of wine was central to such occasions, following the rites of Dionysus, god of wine.

Festivals honouring Dionysus took place throughout the year, and usually involved the generous consumption of the sacred potation that was being celebrated, leading to mass

For the ancient Greeks, the cult of wine drinking followed the rites of Dionysus, the god of wine. This Dutch etching by Jan de Bisschop (1672–1689) depicts a statue of Dionysus holding a wine cup and a bunch of grapes, his left arm wrapped around a satyr with a panther between his legs.

frenzied dancing and phallic rituals. Such celebrations were more than just an excuse for drunkenness and licentiousness. The cult of Dionysus revolved around death and rebirth – the symbolic end of the year and the crushing of the grapes, followed in the spring by the god's return, and the tasting of the new wine.

Wine, associated from its earliest origins with the divine, had become more than just a product to be consumed: it was not even just a gift from the gods, but a sacred libation that connected man with the divine, and perhaps even had the power to make him more god-like.

Enotria, the Land of Vines

The Greeks called the southern part of the Italian peninsula Enotria, or the Land of Vines. Even before the arrival of the Greeks, the mysterious civilization of the Etruscans had sophisticated and well-developed viticulture in place across Etruria, much of what is now central Italy, extending across present-day Tuscany, Umbria and Latium. Vines were cultivated alongside other crops, and it is probable that the system of training vines up trees and other living supports (an agricultural practice still seen in parts of Tuscany today) was undertaken by the Etruscans.

The craft of winemaking was well established. Indeed, in Etruscan hilltop towns such as Volsinii (possibly present-day Orvieto), archaeological evidence demonstrates the sophistication and ingenuity of the ancient winemakers. Intricate caves were hand-dug out of the soft volcanic tufa over three floors. Grapes brought from the vineyards below to the top of the town were crushed and pressed, and the juice was then allowed to flow by gravity along underground stone channels leading

Etruscan *bucchero* wine cup. The fragile complexity of this beautiful wine cup, dating from 620–580 BC, indicates that it would only be used for the most special or sacred occasions.

to large earthenware fermentation vessels. The juice fermented into wine in near ideal, cave-cool conditions and it is probable that the quality of the wines benefited as a result, maintaining fragrance and freshness as well as a slight residual sweetness. Once fermentation was complete, the wine was transferred, again by gravity, to clean earthenware storage vessels deep underground where it could be kept for lengthy periods and improve with age.

The Etruscans were a highly developed commercial and agricultural civilization, and wine was clearly central to their culture. It was a commodity that was enjoyed not just locally but as a valuable object of trade. That wine was central to the Etruscan way of life is evidenced by the extensive examples of Etruscan earthenware that have been discovered by archaeologists, such as the distinctive and characteristic domestic *bucchero* ware, black earthenware pottery in the form of beautifully decorated wine cups and mixing bowls. Splendid ceremonial artefacts, notably examples found in tombs throughout central Italy, further demonstrate the sophistication of the Etruscan civilization as well as the importance of wine in the daily scheme of life and death.

The Romans triumphed over the Etruscans, taking Volsinii and other cities in the Etruscan Confederation by the third century BC. Like all good conquerors, they learned from those that they had vanquished. Indeed, when Volsinii was taken over, the new Roman town of Urbs Vetus carried on the Etruscan methods of winemaking, utilizing the same centuries-old wine cellars. Under the Romans, the resulting wines were traded via the river port of Palianum (where numerous amphorae have been discovered).

By the second century BC, grape growing was an important Roman agricultural activity, and fortunes were made on the production of this valuable commodity. The resulting wines flowed into the capital city to slake the thirst of a population of wealthy citizens eager to enjoy the finer things in life. Everyday beverages made from the fermentation of grapes may have been enjoyed by the masses, but the finest wines were prized and earmarked for those with more patrician tastes – and the money to indulge in them. Indeed, early on, the Romans established the essential link between provenance and quality, the all-encompassing concept of *terroir* that remains a feature of European viticulture today. Wines named after superior areas – falernum and surrentium (both in Campania), albanum (the Alban Hills above Rome), praetutium (on the Adriatic seaboard) or rhaeticum (the wine hills north of Verona), to name but a few of Rome's 'grands crus' – were precious commodities that were able to command elevated prices.

In a wine tavern in Pompeii (of which archaeologists have discovered more than 200), a price list painted on the wall gives some indication of a qualitative pecking order:

> For one *as* you can drink wine,
> For two, you can drink the best,
> For four, you can drink falernum.

By the Roman era, wine was not just for special occasions: it was to be enjoyed by all, plebians and nobility alike. The ruins of Pompeii have revealed that street-side wine taverns were not much different from the bars of today.

Systematic, specialized viticulture was an important element of economic life to the Romans. Lucius Columella wrote a twelve-volume farming treatise, *De Re Rustica*, which covered most aspects of Roman agricultural activities, including the growing of grapes. In this early work, he discusses the positioning of a vineyard, the selection of grape variety, how to lay out and stake the vines, whether to cultivate them up trees or other living supports, even the management of slaves for labour.

To the Romans, wine lay at the heart of culture and civilization. It was a feature of daily life for the rich as well as the poor. Naturally, there were huge differences in wines enjoyed by the various classes in Roman society, from aged vintages from the grands crus vineyards of the ancient world to thin, weak wines suited only to the lower classes. Like the Greeks, the Romans normally drank wines mixed with either water or seawater, and often flavoured them with boiled grape must, honey, herbs or spices.

Old vintages aged for 25 years or longer would have been oxidized. Oxygen would have caused such wines to turn gold, then a deep mahogany brown in colour, though if the wines contained sufficient alcohol, then they would not have spoiled. According to Roman literature, such rare old vintages were prized, with the best vintages lasting for upwards of a hundred years.

The Romans, like the Greeks, it seemed, had a penchant for sweet wines, hence the practice of adding boiled grape must or honey to the finished wine. Another method of making such sticky dessert wines was to harvest the grapes, then leave them out to dry in the sun until they reached an almost raisined state. The sugar-rich, semi-dried grapes would then be pressed and fermented, and as the yeasts could not convert all the natural sugar into alcohol, the wine would retain a residual sweetness that was thickly concentrated.

Roman expansion led to the vine being taken and planted throughout much of its western Empire. The resulting wine served to slake the thirst of the legionnaires while at the same time being introduced to the barbarians who had been conquered, a gift of Roman civilization. Vineyards were planted along Roman supply and trade routes – the Rhône corridor leading through Burgundy to the north; along the Rhine and Mosel Valleys of Germany; around the Mediterranean seaboard to the Iberian peninsula; across the Pannonian Plain that led to Constantinople and the Eastern Empire; and down the Dalmatian coast of Illyricum to Greece. Burdigala (present-day Bordeaux) was an important seaport especially for trade of wine to Britain and the Baltic. And of course the vine was even taken across the channel and planted in the Roman province of Britannia.

Soon wine from the provinces was flowing back to Rome, and the great vineyards of Europe were on their way to becoming well and truly established.

3
The Great Vineyards of Europe

From its earliest roots and origins in Mesopotamia, and over a period of centuries and millennia, *Vitis vinifera* steadily crept its way through Asia Minor into the eastern Mediterranean, and from there rapidly spread across the Greek islands, the Italian peninsula, and eventually across much of Western Europe. Indeed, it was here, more than anywhere else on earth, primarily between the temperate latitudes of 30 and 50 degrees, that the grape vine sent down its deepest roots, thriving in its most propitious and fruitful habitats as well as in areas where its very survival was sometimes only barely marginal at best.

Across Italy, the Iberian peninsula, France, Germany and much of Central Europe, vineyards were established centuries and millennia ago that have historically produced some of the greatest wines in the world, and whose wines, even today, continue to serve as the benchmarks against which all others are judged.

The Origins of Wine Growing
in Western Europe

As Roman influence spread across southern Gaul and the province of Narbonensis and into the Iberian provinces of Tarraconensis, Baetica and Lusitania, so it seems did the cultivation of the wine grape. The Empire expanded across the continent, and wine was needed to quench the seemingly insatiable thirst of its legionnaires. Thus the transport of wine from Rome and its provinces was a necessary and considerable undertaking. Trade routes for the supply not just of wine but also of other essentials from Rome snaked along roads that led up the Rhône Valley to Central France and as far north as Germany, as well as west around the Mediterranean seaboard into Spain, and across southwest France eventually to Burdigala (Bordeaux), from where wine and other trading commodities were shipped by sea to Britain and to the Lowlands.

Within a relatively short period of time, much of Gaul had succumbed to the superior benefits that Roman civilization could offer, not least of which was the production of wine. Since the Mediterranean climate was perfect for the vine, it was not long before it was transplanted to these new Roman provinces. Soon wine was being made, enjoyed locally and even transported back to Rome itself, where it could often undersell the homegrown product. It wasn't just in those lands most suited to its cultivation that the vine thrived: indeed, what is perhaps most surprising was its adaptability to more northern climes and indeed its ability to survive – and to produce superlative results – in those areas where it was planted almost at the very limit of its viability, notably in northern vineyards such as Champagne, and on the steep riverbanks of the Mosel and Rhine rivers in Germany, as

After Carlo Dolci, *Christ with Eucharist*, 1840–1900, chromolithograph. The Christian era charged wine with new and special meaning and significance through the celebration of the Eucharist. Indeed, Christianity, with its constant need for wine to celebrate this daily sacrament, is credited in great measure with the survival of viticulture through the Dark Ages.

well as in alpine habitats such as the Valle d'Aosta and the Südtirol of present-day Italy.

If wine was a gift of Roman civilization that was most readily accepted, the Roman presence was not always universally welcomed. Barbarian invasions from the north were persistent and eventually successful and Europe entered into the Dark Ages. Yet viticulture and the making of wine endured, notably under the protection of the Church. Before the fall of Rome, the Emperor Constantine was the first Christian ruler, and Christianity triumphed in Gaul when the Merovingian Frankish king Clovis was converted in 496, and baptized in the cathedral of Reims, setting a trend that would be followed by later kings of France.

Christianity of course encouraged the production of wine, as it was needed on a daily basis for the celebration of the Eucharist. Furthermore, for many, in an era when reliable clean and fresh water supplies were not always available, wine also became something of a necessity of life even for ordinary people, not just the clergy, the rich or the gentry. Thus, even during the so-called Dark Ages – a period of more than four centuries when Europe had no unifying powers – viniculture, the science of growing grapes and making wine, was never allowed to die out. During periods of chaos, when lawless, pagan, marauding tribes swept across the continent, the study and improvement of viticulture and winemaking continued to be carried out.

Great advances in both viticulture and winemaking were made in Christian monasteries across Europe. The monastic life revolved around prayer and work, and the Benedictine Rule prescribed an ascetic diet which included the consumption of wine as a daily requirement. So the cultivation of vines for the making of wine both as a daily beverage and to celebrate the Eucharist was an essential monastic task. Not surprisingly, monasteries acquired great tracts of land, often bequeathed to them by wealthy benefactors hoping, perhaps, for a more favourable place in heaven.

By the Middle Ages, the Benedictines had extensive vineyard holdings across Burgundy, notably at Gevrey-Chambertin

Dutch mezzotint by Nicolaes Walraven van Haeften (1678–1715).
Wine, at once sacred and for a time a drink only for a privileged elite,
gradually became a beverage to be imbibed and enjoyed by all levels
of society. Indeed, throughout the Middle Ages and beyond, when
water supplies could often be suspect, wine was considered positively
health-giving.

and Vosne-Romanée, while the Cistercians cultivated possibly the most famous walled vineyard in the world, the legendary Clos de Vougeot. The Abbey of Clairvaux, meanwhile, had extensive holdings in Champagne. Schloss Johannisberg and Kloster Eberbach in Germany are two famous wine estates with an illustrious monastic history. Wine-producing monasteries extended through Spain, notably all along the Camino de Santiago, the medieval world's most important pilgrimage route. In Italy, modern winemakers have researched medieval tithes to discover the vineyards from which wines were specified, since the Church would have known – and wanted – only the best wines to be so donated. Even today, there are still monasteries where the cultivation of grapes and the production of wine is carried out by devout monks. And of course monks and missionaries carried the vine with them to the New World.

As repositories of knowledge and learning, monasteries promoted extensive and painstaking research into the cultivation of the grape, for surely the production of the best wines was seen as a way of honouring the glory of God (as well as of satisfying earthly desires). The technology of winemaking was improved by the monks, and medieval monastic cellars were as advanced as any in the world, with immense beam presses and cellars full of wooden vats for the storage of wine. Wine was also a business for monasteries, and efficient monastic supply chains enabled such wines to be enjoyed not only in situ but by discerning clerics beyond the walls of the monastery.

That such tireless monastic work was carried out to the benefit of all is evidenced by the seventeenth-century Benedictine monk Dom Pierre Pérignon, who, in the abbey cellars of Hautvillers, in the Champagne region, worked so diligently to improve the local wines. Pérignon's greatest contribution was his research both in the vineyard, to improve the quality of grapes, and in the cellar, notably through the blending of wines from throughout the region to create a harmonious cuvée. Such meticulous research, carried out during a lifetime of monastic devotion, epitomizes the contributions that the Church made to our enjoyment of wine today.

The roots of the great vineyards of Europe were established, nurtured and cared for in times of plenty as in times of strife. Today we are able to enjoy and appreciate the fruits of our ancestors' considerable labours. Indeed, the legacy of the early pioneers of European viniculture extends in an unbroken line from before the Romans right up to the modern era.

France — the Benchmark

France has long been considered the greatest wine-growing country in the world. Vineyards first planted by the Romans, nurtured by monks or commercially developed by merchant entrepreneurs centuries ago today still produce wines that are by any standard the benchmarks against which all others are measured.

Bordeaux, the centre of the wine trade since the era when it was the Roman port of Burdigala, is still today considered by many to be the world's greatest wine region. The Roman poet Ausonius came from Burdigala and wrote of his homeland overgrown with vines. During the Middle Ages, wine production increased along the Dordogne and Garonne Valleys, as well as across Blaye, Bourg and the Graves. The region and its wines gained a further commercial boost when in 1152 Eleanor of Aquitaine married Henry Plantagenet, later to become King of England. Numerous privileges were granted to the winegrowers, and the wines of Bordeaux were soon flowing into London – thus beginning the romance of the English with their beloved claret, which continues to this day.

The great vineyards of France remain benchmarks against which all others have traditionally been measured. Famous and historic properties such as Château Margaux, in Bordeaux's Médoc, produce wines that are amongst the most prestigious and sought-after in the world.

Bordeaux, both historically and currently, is primarily known as the source of red wines produced from cabernet sauvignon, cabernet franc and merlot grapes. Such wines have become models for a host of varietals made from these same grapes grown all around the world. Yet claret – the English name for red bordeaux wine – remains, in many eyes, supreme, not least because its greatest wines, the classified premiers crus or first-growth wines such as château margaux, château lafite-rothschild, château latour, château mouton-rothschild and château haut-brion, are consistently able to command prices *en primeur* – before they have even been bottled and released from the wine estates – that are still always among the highest in the world. Apart from this exalted elite, there are scores of other *crus classés* – classified wines – such as st emilion, as well as unclassified wines such as pomerol that are consistently in the highest demand amongst connoisseurs (witness château pétrus, unclassified but one of the most highly sought – and expensive – wines in the world).

An argument can be made that Bordeaux is the world's greatest wine region not only because it produces some of the world's greatest and most expensive wines, but also because it is the unstinting source of such a vast range of wines of all styles and at all quality levels. White bordeaux, produced primarily from sémillon and sauvignon blanc grapes, can reach exalted heights, notably in the Graves, while plentiful and accessible wines come from Entre-Deux-Mers and elsewhere.

Meanwhile, in the small wine enclaves of Sauternes and Barsac, remarkable sweet white dessert wines are produced from sémillon, sauvignon blanc and muscadelle grapes that are attacked by *Botrytis cinerea*, known also as noble rot, a natural process that concentrates grape sugar and aromas to result in astonishing, intense and honeyed marvels. Château d'Yquem is the most famous wine estate and indeed dessert wines have been produced here since at least the eighteenth century and possibly even earlier.

Cabernet sauvignon and merlot are cultivated elsewhere in France, in many cases with great success, notably in the Languedoc and Provence. But nowhere else in France do such wines reach the exalted heights that they do in Bordeaux. Indeed, one particularly interesting part of the development of viticulture in France is the way that, through trial and error over the centuries, certain grape varieties have come to thrive particularly well and to be associated with specific wine regions and not with others.

Burgundy, located in eastern France, is another wine region of great renown that has long historical antecedents. It is possible that the ancient Celts were cultivating the vine even before the Romans conquered Gaul in 51 BC. After the fall of the Roman Empire, the Merovingians continued to cultivate vineyards and the wines from Burgundy were highly praised.

From about the sixth century on, abbeys, priories and monasteries were founded in the region, and over the centuries these ecclesiastical orders acquired vast tracts of valuable land, constructing buildings where wines could be made and cellars where they could be stored. For many orders, manual work was part of the monastic rule and indeed such devotion was considered to be part of a spiritual journey. Thus a systematic approach to growing grapes as well as making wine was carried out by the Benedictines of Cluny as well as the Cistercian order that was based at Cîteaux, near modern Nuits-St-Georges. Renowned vineyards such as the Clos de Vougeot, La Romanée, La Tâche and others can all be traced to monastic origins. Charlemagne, king of the Franks, meanwhile, is commemorated in the great white burgundy corton-charlemagne as the grapes come from a plot of land that he donated to the Abbey of Saulieu in 775.

Burgundy, like Bordeaux, is the source of outstanding red as well white wines. If the cabernets and merlot are the great red grapes of Bordeaux, in Burgundy pinot noir reigns supreme. Apart from limited amounts of gamay, no other red grapes are cultivated here. Why? Pinot noir, it has been accepted for centuries, is the grape variety most able to express itself in the celebrated vineyards of the Côte d'Or. Indeed, the French concept of *terroir* and the concern with producing wines uniquely typical of a locality or region is so ingrained that it would seem absurd even to consider planting anything else.

Such steadfastness means that Burgundy is thus able to present its own archetypal wines that have become models: voluptuous, silky reds produced almost exclusively from the pinot noir grape, and rich, concentrated, sometimes barrel-fermented whites from chardonnay, a grape that is indigenous to the region, but which has since gone on to be planted throughout the world.

Pinot noir is a notoriously temperamental and difficult grape to cultivate, yet, when and where it ripens fully, it is able to give results that are astonishing and sublime. Nowhere is *terroir* more fittingly demonstrated than in the region of Burgundy, where the character of one finished wine can be totally different from that of another wine made from the same grape variety cultivated on an adjacent plot of land. Here, to reflect such variations, historical precedence has resulted in the land itself being classified precisely into ever more specific appellations, moving from the regional bourgogne AOC to ever more exact designations that indicate increasing quality and individuality.

Under such a system, the grape variety does not need to be stated anywhere on the label. For red burgundy from the classic heartland is always pure pinot noir: it cannot be anything else. Similarly, white burgundy is 100 per cent chardonnay, though that ubiquitous grape name never need be mentioned on the wine label (the only time you will see chardonnay on the label of a white burgundy is if the wine comes from the wine commune of Chardonnay itself, the town that gives its name to the grape variety).

Like the region's most exalted red wines, the greatest white burgundies may have ever more precise appellations as well as classifications into premiers and grands crus. Wines from communes such as Meursault and Puligny-Montrachet are highly sought, while grands crus such as le montrachet, from a single classified vineyard, are by many considered the pinnacle of all white wines. Chablis, a small wine island to the north of Dijon, meanwhile, is another Burgundian wine zone famous for its chardonnay wines, and with its own very precise hierarchy of premier and grand cru wines.

The famous Burgundian walled vineyard known as the Clos du Vougeot can be traced back to monastic origins.

Though pinot noir and chardonnay reign supreme in Burgundy to produce benchmark reds and whites admired (and copied) around the world, these same two grapes also thrive to the north, on the gently undulating chalk hills of Champagne, to produce what is still regarded as the world's greatest sparkling wine.

Vineyards were certainly here around the time of St Rémi, the bishop of Reims who baptized Clovis i, king of the Franks, in AD 496. It is probable that by this date wines were already being stored in the vast underground *crayères* – galleries that had been carved by the Romans out of the same soft chalk terrain that nourishes the vines. But Champagne, the sparkling wine as we know it, is a relatively recent arrival. Of course, in this far northern vineyard, it is quite possible that in wines stored in cool chalk caves deep underground the fermentation might have been stopped before all the fermentable sugars had been converted to alcohol. Once the wines were brought back up to ground level, or else in the transition from cold winter to warmer spring temperatures, fermentation might recommence, causing carbon dioxide, or bubbles, as a by-product. However, until the invention of bottles strong enough to withstand the pressure, there was no way for this effervescence to be captured.

Again, we look to the monasteries for the perfection of this unique wine. Indeed, it was at the Abbey of Hautvillers where Dom Pierre Pérignon and his fellow monks perfected methods of making sparkling wines systematically and safely. By tying down corked bottles with string, the carbon dioxide that was a result of secondary fermentation in the bottle was trapped in the wine. 'Brothers, come quickly! I am drinking stars,' the blind cellarmaster is reputed to have cried.

Champagne can only be produced in Champagne, a protected name that defines both the territory from which the wine comes as well as the unique process for rendering still wines sparkling. Other regions in the world may try to emulate it, planting pinot noir and chardonnay, carefully blending cuvées, and following the process of secondary fermentation in the bottle. Yet champagne remains unique, a combination of the particular characteristics of a far northern vineyard where grapes are cultivated at the limit of their viability, the profound chalk soil in which they are nourished, the cool underground *caves* carved out of that same chalk, and literally centuries of expertise in the selection of grapes, blending of wines from a number of vineyards and even vintages, winemaking, maturing and marketing.

The Rhône Valley has historically been a natural avenue for trade and commerce, and has been populated for millennia. The Greek Phocaeans founded Massilia (Marseille) in 600 BC, brought the vine with them and established trading communities to the north. After the Greeks, the Romans came, saw and conquered all, leaving behind great monuments of ancient civilization, such as the amphitheatre and triumphal arch at Orange, patrician villas at Vaison-la-Romaine, temples at Vienne and much else. The wines of the Rhône were extolled by ancient writers such as Pliny and Martial.

After the Romans left, the Church kept alive viticulture during the Dark Ages. Much later, when the papal seat was transferred to Avignon in 1308, the wines of the southern Rhône received an even greater boost through papal patronage when Châteauneuf-du-Pape became the summer residence of the popes.

Today the wines of the Rhône Valley remain classics. The southern Rhône is the source of wines produced from a cocktail of different grape varieties in varying proportions, both red and white, from vineyards at Châteauneuf-du-Pape, Gigondas, Vacqueyras, Sablet, Rasteau and elsewhere.

The world's most famous sparkling wine, Champagne, owes a debt to the blind cellarmaster Dom Pierre Pérignon, who helped to perfect the method of producing sparkling wines by secondary fermentation in the bottle. This statue of the monk stands at the entrance to the famous cellars of Möet et Chandon.

A typical *winstub* in Alsace encapsulates elements of both French and German wine culture: wines are made from German grape varieties such as riesling and gewürztraminer yet vinified in the classic French style to be enjoyed with food.

Fine, forceful rosés come from Tavel and Lirac. The northern Rhône, meanwhile, yields great and powerful wines produced primarily from syrah cultivated on the extraordinarily well-exposed hill of Hermitage, at Cornas and St Joseph and, further north, over the baked slopes of the Côte Rôtie just below Vienne. The northern Rhône is also the source of fabulous compact and concentrated white wines that can be remarkably long-lived, notably white hermitage (from marsanne and roussanne grapes) and condrieu, made in miniscule quantities from the characterful and more delicate viognier, a grape variety of immense character that in recent decades has been widely planted elsewhere.

Wine sometimes is as much a product of history as of *terroir*. Witness Alsace, a region that has see-sawed numerous times between France and Germany. A part of France since the end of the First World War, the region even today still seems poised in limbo between the Rhine and the Vosges mountains: the cuisine combines elements from both countries; the picturesque half-timbered architecture appears Germanic; the region has its own language that is neither French nor German; and its range of wines are produced from German grape varieties vinified in the classic French style. Indeed, riesling d'alsace, fine, fragrant, with a steely, bone-dry backbone, has inspired winemakers in Australia, California and New Zealand to attempt to make this racy, exciting dry style that combines aroma with body and structure.

Elsewhere, sauvignon blanc grapes grown in the vineyards of the Upper Loire, notably around Sancerre and Pouilly-sur-Loire, result in classic, intensely aromatic wines that are the inspiration for sauvignon wines from New Zealand, South Africa, California and elsewhere. The previously mentioned powerful, chunky syrah-based wines of the northern Rhône similarly provide something of a model for blockbuster shiraz wines produced in Australia. Meanwhile, beaujolais nouveau is the quintessential 'new' wine, produced by a unique process of whole-grape fermentation that results in fruity, gluggable wines that can be enjoyed just weeks after the harvest. And of course great, concentrated, honeyed dessert wines such as those from Sauternes, Barsac, Monbazillac and the Loire Valley, produced from grapes affected by *Botrytis cinerea*, are touchstone dessert wines that rank among the greatest wines in the world – and the most expensive.

France is also an abundant source of scores of lesser wines that are well made, interesting, high quality and contrasting in style, from the light and ethereal mountain wines of the Savoie, and the generous and relatively inexpensive wines of Languedoc and Provence, to the robust, fortified *vin doux naturels* of Banyuls and Roussillon. *Vins de pays*, or country wines, are widely produced throughout France and an ever-increasing trend is to market such wines varietally – by grape name – as well as by brand, a trend that moves away from the traditional Gallic reliance on *terroir*.

Whatever happens in the future, I think that France will long continue to be considered the greatest wine-producing country in the world. Nowhere else on earth is able to give the world both exalted classics that serve as the benchmarks against which wines from elsewhere are measured, and more accessible wines that can be enjoyed at all levels.

The Iberian Peninsula

The Phoenicians may have been the first to carry the vine with them to their outpost in Cádiz, a city founded in 1100 BC. There it is probable that they set down roots for the vineyards that today produce sherry, one of the great fortified wines of the world. These intrepid seafarers furthermore explored elsewhere in the Iberian peninsula, so it is probable that they carried the vine with them up the Tagus and Douro rivers, and even as far inland as the Ebro that leads to the wine country of Rioja.

When the Romans colonized the peninsula, they planted further vineyards across the provinces of Tarraconensis, Baetica and Lusitania. Cenicero, in the Rioja region, was a Roman outpost and archaeological evidence has shown that wines have been produced here for at least 2,000 years.

As the Roman Empire gradually fell apart and the barbarians from the north moved in, viticulture continued, and indeed was still in place by the time of the Moorish occupation of the Iberian peninsula in AD 711. Though the Koran forbade the use of wine, trade in wine continued, with England in particular importing large quantities. The Moors were cultured rulers who, like the Romans, brought great civilizing benefits and who were also more than happy to let the locals continue to live their lives and carry on local tradition and culture.

Yet if the Moors were enlightened rulers, opposition remained. The *Reconquista* was a struggle to expel the Moors that continued over the centuries, until gradually, almost piece by piece, Spain was finally reclaimed by Christians. In January 1492 the last emir was forced to surrender the Moors' most splendid outpost at Granada, marking the end of the 700-year-old Moorish occupation of Spain and Portugal. It was, of course, the same year that Christopher Columbus set sail from Andalusia across the Atlantic to discover a new world.

In the centuries that followed, Spanish wine, most notably sack from the sherry region or the Canary Islands, gained a considerable following, especially in England. Its greatest champion was Shakespeare's magnificent character Sir John Falstaff who, in *Henry IV Part 2*, declares: 'If I had a thousand sons, the first humane principle I would teach them should be, to forswear thin potations and to addict themselves to sack.'

Even today, the most famous wines from the Iberian peninsula are probably still the great fortified duo of sherry and port. Both are historic wines that were undoubtedly vinous creations developed primarily for export markets rather than to meet local or national demand. Such fortified wines, it was discovered, were robust enough to stand up to lengthy voyages by sea, and the sweeter styles of wine appealed to the British and the Dutch, who especially enjoyed such strong and warming drinks. Politics came into such trade, too. In 1703 Britain and Portugal signed the Methuen Treaty that led to an exchange of English woollens for port wine. This allowed English merchants to take a commanding position in the Portuguese wine trade and some of the great port dynasties were founded during this period.

Historical events, it seems, have often had a large part to play in the development of wine. In medieval times, the most significant pilgrimage route in Europe was the Camino de Santiago, which led to Santiago de Compostela, where the remains of St James were reputed to have been washed ashore. The pilgrims entered Spain from France by two principal routes, the Roncesvalles Pass in Navarra and the Puerto de Somport in neighbouring Aragón. This great trans-European thoroughfare saw the passing of literally millions who saw it as both a duty and the adventure of a lifetime to make the arduous journey to the tomb of St James. Churches, hospitals, monasteries and inns sprang up all along the well-travelled routes, which passed through Navarra and Rioja before continuing on eventually to Galicia. The pilgrims needed places to stay overnight, and of course they required food and drink. Thus a medieval tourist industry grew up to serve their needs, not least with the provision of wine to slake an immense collective thirst that arose from walking along this dusty, ancient thoroughfare.

It is conjectured that Burgundian monks, en route to Santiago, came to Rioja, found the region suitable for the cultivation of grapes, and settled there to cultivate vineyards and make wine, bringing with them sophisticated French winemaking techniques, notably for the storage and maturation of red wines in oak barrels. Such wines, however, would hardly have been produced in such fashion to slake the thirst of the vast mass of pilgrims, who most certainly would have chosen to drink the youngest and cheapest *vinos jóvenes* – young wines from the latest harvest. More than likely, the fashion for oak-aged rioja arose much later, when the region was able to step in to supply French markets with such wines after the vineyards of France were first struck down by a particularly virulent form of oidium, and later by *Phylloxera*, the ravaging aphid that eventually went on to destroy almost all the vineyards of Europe. It was during this period, before *Phylloxera* came to Spain, that Rioja was able to emerge as the most significant region for quality red Spanish table wines. This is a position it still holds today, though other areas now vie with it for supremacy, notably Ribeira del Duero and Catalunya.

Since the fall of Franco, Spain has emerged from the shadow of the dictatorship, developed a thriving modern economy and taken its place at the centre of Europe. The wine industry has benefited greatly and a more modern approach to winemaking and wine marketing is now in place. Fine wines produced with the most modern technology are coming out of Galicia (notably albariño whites), Catalunya (fine red, white and sparkling), Castilla y Léon (outstanding, world-class reds) and the Mediterranean seaboard.

Even the vast central interior, Castilla-La Mancha, has shown itself capable of producing quality wines that are well made and well priced. In this arid and treeless highland, where there was little wood but plenty of clay, the wines were traditionally fermented in immense earthenware *tinajas* – great amphora-shaped vessels that were directly descended from the earthernware fermentation *dolia* found throughout the Roman wine world. Villarrobledo was long the principal town for the production of *tinajas*. Not only was there a plentiful supply of clay, but the local potters had maintained the centuries-old skills needed for their manufacture, while the town still had kilns large enough to fire them. However, the relatively recent advent of stainless-steel, temperature-controlled vats has seen *tinajas* fall by the way as the Spanish wine industry has modernized at speed. Thus the particular stone taste of valdepeñas wine fermented in earthernware *tinajas* – a taste I

In central Spain, where wood is scarce but clay plentiful, wines were traditionally fermented in earthenware *tinajas*, huge vessels that are direct descendants of the Roman earthenware fermentation vessels used since ancient times.

remember from as recently as the 1980s and '90s – is sadly no more.

Similarly, if barrels or casks were not the usual vessels for fermentation in the treeless interior of Spain, neither were they always used for the transport of wine. Rather, the vast herds of sheep, pigs and goats that grazed across Spain's endless interior resulted in the use of *pellejos* or *borrachos* for the storage and transport of wine. These sheep, pig or goatskin receptacles were made from the tanned hide of the whole animal, feet and all, sewn together inside-out, and lined with pitch to make them liquid-tight. They could contain around 60 litres or more and could be conveniently carried over the shoulders of a strong man by gripping the wineskins by the animals' forelegs. Leather *botas*, also hair-side in and lined with pitch, served as personal wineskins for the people of the Spanish interior, a familiar receptacle carried out to the fields, the *bota* held up high and squeezed so that the wine hissed satisfyingly into the back of the throat.

In truth, who knows what the wine contained within those pitch-lined animal skins generally tasted like? Surely the taint of animal would have overpowered even the most robust wines. Today these picturesque methods are no more. Spain is a wholly modern country that makes use of the most up-to-date technologies to result in a range of outstanding wines at all levels. Modern technology, intelligently applied to fruit cultivated and harvested wisely, may now allow for sound and sometimes outstanding wines to be produced just about anywhere the grape vine grows. But inevitably something of the romance may have gone.

Portugal, like its neighbour Spain, has always had a strong winegrowing tradition, dating back at least as far as the time of the Roman Empire, when legionnaires crossed the Lima River in the far north of the country and chose to settle there, so beautiful and fertile a land did they find. Indeed, it was probably the Romans who introduced the bucolic method of training vines up trees and other living supports to free the land below for other crops. This method of cultivation was still widely in place in the Minho as recently as twenty years ago.

Portugal the country, like its wines, has tended to keep itself to itself. With the exception of some global brands, and of course port, its wines have mainly been made and enjoyed by the Portuguese themselves. Produced primarily from indigenous grape varieties not encountered anywhere else, distinctive characterful table wines ranging from the everyday to exalted vintages collected by connoisseurs are today being produced in the Alentejo, Ribatejo, Estremadura, Dão, Beiras, Douro, Bairrada, Colares and elsewhere.

Those Roman-inspired vineyards growing up trees in the Minho have long been the source of distinctive, light *vinhos verdes* – 'green wines', the term used to designate such wines from the Minho region (though confusingly they can be either white, rosé or red). The best examples are refreshing and delightful, especially those produced from characterful indigenous grapes such as alvarinho (the same grape as albariño from across the border in Galicia) and loureiro.

Port wine is one of the country's most famous exports. It is a fortified wine made from grapes grown and processed in the demarcated Douro Valley wine zone. Port appears in an array of styles, most usually red but also white, and from dry, semi-dry to sweet, and from wines aged for lengthy periods in wooden casks to vintage and crusted ports aged in the bottle for decades. Many of the port lodges of Vila Nova de Gaia, opposite the town of Porto, were founded in the seventeenth century and family port dynasties still remain, producing a wine that is often imitated elsewhere in the world but rarely equalled. Indeed, this is one of the oldest protected demarcated wine regions in the world, with wine laws established as long ago as 1756 to protect the authenticity and origin of the product. Vintage port is one of the great wines of the world, capable of combining immense power and complexity with voluptuous, silky, richly sweet smoothness.

Another of the world's great historic fortified wines, madeira, comes from the Portuguese island in the Atlantic Ocean off the African coast. The island's strategic position made it a port of call for traders en route across the Atlantic to North or South America, as well as to Africa, or around the Cape of Good Hope to sea routes to India and the Far East. Ships would call in to replenish provisions before such long sea voyages, not least to stock up with wine both to serve as ballast in the holds of the ships and for consumption and trade on arrival at their destinations. However, since the wine had to cross the Equator, it often spoiled, becoming oxidized or turning to vinegar. One way to stop this was to fortify it with the addition of a strong distilled spirit made from cane sugar.

So fortified, the wines became virtually indestructible and it seems the sea voyages in which they had to endure the hellish equatorial heat as well as the rough churning of the sea passage seemed only to improve them. Therefore, once the wines no longer needed to endure lengthy sea journeys, the local industry eventually found a way to replicate the conditions by ageing the wine in *estufas*, heated rooms which helped the wines to madeirize, concentrating flavours and allowing them to gain colour as well as complexity.

One other important Portuguese contribution to the world of wine should not be overlooked. The country is still the world's main source of what until just a few decades ago was indispensable for the production of fine wine, the natural cork. New forms of closure may be becoming ever more popular, but it seems probable that the best wines, especially those destined for lengthy ageing, will continue to require fine-quality natural corks to close the bottle, and Portugal is still the very best source for them.

Italy, a Rich Vinous Patrimony

Wine is produced in every single one of Italy's twenty regions. From the snow-covered Alps of the Valle d'Aosta, where Europe's highest vineyards are located, way down to Pantelleria, the tiny volcanic island located between Sicily and North Africa, the vine thrives, and is cultivated to produce an amazing array of wines.

If, over millennia, the production of wine has uniquely revealed the particular creative genius of mankind, then the variety and types of wine produced by the ancient Romans is testimony to this. In tufa caves dug deep underground they were able to practise cool-temperature fermentation; wines were sweetened with boiled grape must and de-acidified with the addition of chalk. Wonderful dessert wines were made by semi-drying the grapes until they were nearly raisins (a process still used in Italy today to make *passito* wines). Other Roman practices included mixing wines with seawater and with honey and spices. Rudimentary sparkling wines were made by sealing still-fermenting wines in amphorae with cork stoppers and pitch and keeping them stored in cool seawater, thus causing carbon dioxide to remain trapped within the wine, and so contributing effervescence.

The concept of *terroir* that is such a fundamental underlying principle for European winegrowers was certainly understood by the Romans. Lands were classified by soil, elevation and aspect. Some grape varieties were deemed suitable to be grown in certain conditions, while others were forbidden.

If the colonies, notably Gallia and Hispania, later supplied Rome's thirsty citizens with their basic everyday wines, there was most certainly a pecking order. Indeed, iconic wines such as falernian, albanum, surrentium and rhaeticum were as prized by connoisseurs as the great growths of Bordeaux and Burgundy are today. Not only were such Roman grands crus aged for upwards of decades, but they must also have fetched prices that were little short of fantastic, even by today's standards.

After the decline of the Roman Empire, Italy, like the rest of Europe, entered the Dark Ages as the Goths and Lombards descended from the north. The civilizing cosmopolitan influences that the Romans had provided were replaced by a more inward-looking society based on feudal systems of agriculture. Through much of the medieval and Renaissance periods that followed, the peninsula was fragmented into independent city-states, kingdoms, principalities and republics ruled by Genoa, Venice, Florence, Siena, the Habsburgs, the Spanish Bourbons and of course the Vatican. Indeed, Italy was not to regain a sense of nationality until it was unified in 1861. This is probably one reason why allegiance remains so strong to the local and the regional.

Through the Renaissance, the aristocracy and the nouveau-riche class of bankers, merchants and traders most certainly provided a market for good wines. Indeed some of Italy's best-known (and best) wine producers today, such as the Antinori and Frescobaldi families of Tuscany, can trace their antecedents back to the fourteenth century or earlier. Meanwhile, for the ordinary people, wine grapes were just another agricultural commodity, and simple everyday wine was part of a quotidian diet based on olive oil and bread, the staples of the Mediterranean.

As in France, the traditions of winemaking were kept alive in the monasteries and other religious institutions. Wine was

The drying of grapes to a near-raisin state to preserve and concentrate grape sugars is a method of winemaking that dates back to the ancient era. Such *passito* wines are still produced in Italy today.

of course a central element in the celebration of the Eucharist. As the Church grew ever more wealthy, with the Vatican rivalling even secular powers, prelates enjoyed the good life and the pleasures of the flesh were to be embraced, not denied. Indeed, priests, bishops, archbishops and popes were not averse to the enjoyment of fine wine, as well as food. As previously mentioned, an examination of medieval and Renaissance church records, for example, has revealed the stipulation of tithes with reference to wines from specific vineyards: for indeed the priests knew always which vineyards yielded the best wines – and were keen to ensure that they would be the ones to enjoy them.

Yet, if the Greeks, the Etruscans, the Romans, and Renaissance bankers and priests alike appreciated the finest wines on offer across the Italian peninsula, somewhere along the way this rich vinous patrimony was lost. What is particularly surprising is to discover how very recent is the concept of quality wines in modern Italy. Indeed, even up until the 1960s and '70s, the growing of grapes was very much carried out like any other agricultural activity, with a successful harvest measured by the quantity brought in rather than the quality of the fruit. Under a medieval form of sharecropping known as the *mezzadria*, whereby tenant farmers received a house and land to cultivate in exchange for giving half the produce to the *padrone*, the landowner, there was little incentive to produce less fruit of a higher quality. The *mezzadria* was only phased out in central Italy in the 1960s and its legacy continued well into the next decade.

It was only around this time that landowners and winegrowers began to revalue their patrimony. Sassicaia was the first Tuscan wine to take the world by storm, a wine made atypically from the classic French grape varieties cabernet sauvignon, cabernet franc and merlot, aged in new French oak. Tignanello, made from Tuscany's great indigenous grape sangiovese with the addition of some cabernet sauvignon, soon followed and its immediate success spawned an entirely new generation of so-called 'super-Tuscans'. These were sleek, designer wines with hefty price tags. And they proved to the world that Italy was indeed capable of producing world-class wines of the highest quality, style – and price.

Since the 1970s, winegrowers throughout the country have taken to the task of renovating vineyards, reducing yields and working to produce quality wines from a glorious if sometimes bewildering selection of mainly indigenous grape varieties.

Chianti classico changed its historic discipline, eschewing the mandatory use of white grapes in the blend, and the result is better and better wines. Brunello di montalcino, another Tuscan classic and one of the most famous of all Italian wines, is another example of a wine that has improved beyond recognition in recent decades, made by more modern methods that emphasize fruit and suppleness at the expense of lengthy ageing in old wooden casks.

Northwest Italy has long been the source of some of Italy's greatest and most aristocratic red wines. The Piedmontese House of Savoy came to rule over the newly formed Kingdom of Italy following the Risorgimento, and barolo and barbaresco were – and are – certainly wines fitting for kings. Today the wine regions that centre on Le Langhe around the wine town of Alba continue to produce both traditional wines from grapes such as nebbiolo, barbera and dolcetto, as well as smaller quantities of new-wave 'designer' wines from high-profile producers utilizing French grapes such as cabernet sauvignon and chardonnay.

If international grape varieties have sometimes gained the limelight in recent years, what remains most striking about

Italy is its steadfast loyalty to local and regional taste. Grape varieties may be found in one region or locality and nowhere else. Verdicchio is one of Italy's greatest white grapes, yet it is only cultivated in the region of Le Marche. Tocai friulano, another grape variety capable of producing magnificent white wines, appears only in the wine hills of Friuli. Vernaccia, Tuscany's greatest indigenous white grape, is not just unique to that region, but also only cultivated in the calcareous soil around the medieval town of San Gimignano, and nowhere else (other wines produced may bear the same name but, confusingly, refer to wholly different and unique grapes). The ancient sagrantino grape is found exclusively around the town of Montefalco, in Umbria. Why? Its taste is robustly rasping, wholly individual and particular, and in Italy, preference for the very local remains extremely strong. In Tuscany, people from Florence might rarely drink a wine from the neighbouring province of Siena; in Piedmont, those who live in Alba will enjoy barbera d'alba with their *risotto ai funghi* but rarely barbera d'asti, produced just up the road.

There are hundreds if not thousands of indigenous grape varieties grown throughout Italy, many of which are little known outside their locality or region. Grape varieties such as aglianico and greco are more widely encountered throughout the south, their names indicating ancient Hellenic origins. But what about grape varieties such as corvina, raboso and refosco from the Veneto; falanghina and fiano from Campania; arneis, grignolino and favorita from Piedmont; negroamaro and primitivo from Puglia; galioppo from Calabria; montepulciano from Abruzzo; nero d'avola, catarratto and grillo from Sicily; sagrantino and grechetto from Umbria; vermentino from Liguria; bonarda from Lombardy; lagrein and marzemino from Trentino-Alto Adige; picolit from Friuli; pagadebit from Emilia-Romagna; cesanese from Latium; and cannonau and

In Italy, wine has long been considered an agricultural commodity to be purchased in bulk in *damigiane* – 54-litre demi-johns. The wines would then be transferred to more convenient-sized bottles at home, often sealed simply with a layer of oil to keep oxygen at bay since they would be consumed almost immediately.

The concept of fine wine is relatively recent in Italy, with so-called 'super-Tuscan' wines such as Tignanello emerging only in the 1970s. Such wines can be made from either indigenous or international grape varieties, and are almost always matured in new French oak barrels, as here in the cellars of Marchesi Antinori.

monica from Sardinia, to name but a few of Italy's most characterful indigenous grapes? None of these may yet be a household name, but in a wine world increasingly dominated by just a handful of international grape varieties, such examples represent nothing less than a magnificent vinous patrimony that should be protected, supported and celebrated.

Finally, as an interesting historical footnote, in recent years there has been a return to producing wines as they originally had been since Roman times and far earlier: through fermentation not in stainless steel, not in wooden vats or barrels, but in terracotta amphorae buried underground. At opposite ends of the country, Josko Gravner, in Friuli, and the Azienda Agricola Cos in Eastern Sicily, are producing fascinating wines of great purity and typicity that demonstrate not only that the ancient ways are still valid, but also that there is a long continuity over millennia that connects us directly with our ancestors: indeed, we can drink the past!

Germany

The vine is normally considered a Mediterranean plant, most at home in those hot lands where the olive tree also thrives. Yet in northern Europe, way up in Germany's Rhineland, the vine has been successfully cultivated since at least Roman days. I wonder: two thousand years ago, was the climate that much warmer to encourage the cultivation of the vine? Or did the Romans discover all that time ago that the steep and precipitous slopes of Germany's Rhineland – those lands watered by the Rhine and Mosel rivers and their tributaries – had the potential to produce exciting, racy wines that are capable of combining a rare balance of ripeness and fruity acidity, resulting in firm and fruity wines that can be among the most elegant and seductive in the world?

It is probable that the vine was carried here, as it was almost everywhere in the Roman Empire, as a gift of civilization. The Rhine marked the frontier between the Empire to the west and the barbarian Germanic tribes to the east. Trier, Germany's oldest city and located on the Mosel, was a Roman garrison town. The emperor Probus, who ruled from AD 276 to 282, and who helped to strengthen the Rhine and Danube frontiers, is generally credited with introducing viticulture to Germany, though the first written record comes a hundred years later, by the Roman author Ausonius of Bordeaux, in his poem *Mosella*.

The vine, it seems, spread with the expansion of Christianity. Charlemagne encouraged the cultivation of the vine and supported churches and monasteries, with vineyards cultivated to make wine for everyday consumption as well as for holy sacrament. Through the Middle Ages, some of Germany's most important vineyards were established in abbeys and monasteries, notably the Benedictine monastery in the Rheingau that later became Schloss Johannisberg, the estate that is credited with producing the first German wines from grapes affected by noble rot in the eighteenth century. Kloster Eberbach, originally a Cistercian monastery, is today the headquarters of the German Wine Academy.

What were these historic German wines like? It is difficult to say. The Roman poet Venantius Fortunatus writes about German red wine in the sixth century, but it is not until several centuries later that Germany's most famous grape, riesling, is first documented in 1435. The Germans have long seemed to have a predilection for wines made from aromatic varieties, with grapes such as muscat and traminer planted alongside riesling. It seems that there was also a taste for spiced wines that were sometimes fortified.

Germany's vineyards have suffered over the centuries due to the ravages of war. From the Thirty Years War in the early seventeenth century through the two world wars of the twentieth, the wine industry was devastated as vineyards were destroyed by fighting, men were compelled or conscripted to fight, and both domestic and export markets shrank to virtually nothing. Since the second half of the twentieth century, however, the German wine industry has expanded considerably, vineyards have been restructured and the German Wine Law was introduced in 1971. This law not only led to the registration of all vineyards, but also defined quality levels based on the ripeness of grapes. These range from the simple *Deutscher Tafelwein* through quality levels that indicate not only a specified region (qbA) but also increasingly higher degrees of ripeness (qmp), with levels of ripeness indicated by distinctions such as *Kabinett*, *Spätlese*, *Auslese*, *Beerenauslese*, *Eiswein* and *Trockenbeerenauslese*. Such designations, based on sugar levels, usually (though not always) indicate increasing levels of sweetness.

Throughout Germany, though numerous grape varieties are cultivated, the aristocratic if temperamental riesling grape reigns supreme across a number of designated wine regions. The Mosel-Saar-Ruwer is the source of some of the country's most distinctive quality wines. In the Mittelmosel, above wine towns such as Bernkastel, riesling grapes are cultivated on high, south-facing vineyards on slopes covered in scraggy grey slate, with the river far below. In this rarefied environment, the riesling grapes can bask in the afternoon sun, and on chilly nights, the vines are warmed by heat that radiates from the stony ground, resulting in wines that combine scent and fruit with a steely backbone of acidity. The best German wines come from single-estate producers and from precisely named single vineyards, such as the famous Bernkasteler Doktor.

In the Rheingau, between Rüdesheim and Hochheim, vineyards stretch over a gentler and more fertile land, yielding riesling grapes that produce wines with a concentrated and magnificent depth of flavour, fruit and a complex, intriguing elegance. When autumn mists rise from the Rhine, the ideal conditions are created for the production of some of Germany's – and the world's – greatest wines. For such damp mists, followed by warm afternoon sunshine, result in *Edelfäule* or *Botrytis cinerea*, the noble rot that also occurs in Bordeaux's Sauternes region,

The steep slate slopes of Germany's Mosel river provide ideal conditions for the ripening of the temperamental riesling grape.

in the Loire Valley and in Austria's Burgenland. *Edelfäule* concentrates natural grape sugars and contributes rare, haunting, honeyed aromas.

In addition to riesling, numerous less temperamental grape varieties are cultivated in German vineyards. Grapes such as silvaner, which yields nearly twice as much as riesling, and müller-thurgau, a cross between riesling and silvaner, flourish easily. In Rheinhessen, the soil is fertile and the climate more mild, and such grapes are the source of an abundance of soft, fruity, easy-drinking wines, some of which find their ways into commercial blends such as liebfraumilch.

Further south still, in the upper Rhenish lowlands that lead to the slopes of the Haardt mountains, the Rheinpfalz is a hot, bright land that seems almost Mediterranean in character. Fig and palm trees grow in the Rheinpfalz in addition to the vine. Not surprisingly, wines made from distinctive grape varieties such as ruländer, scheurebe and morio-muskat are sensuous and spicy in character, while in the finest vineyards located in the Mittelhaardt, the classic riesling ripens to a deep and rich state, resulting in wines that are at once fiery and exceedingly fine.

Each of Germany's wine areas produces wines that are unique and individual expressions of the land. The tiny Nahe Valley, which flows into the Rhine, yields elegant, golden-tinged wines that seem almost to match the colour of the sun-baked sandstone terraces where the vine thrives. The Kaiserstuhl wines of Baden gain their pithy, fierce character from grapes grown on an outcrop of rich volcanic tufa alongside Germany's Schwarzwald (Black Forest). Dry, piquant silvaner from Franconia, bottled in the distinctive flagon-shaped *bocksbeutel* (the bottle shape is reputed to resemble a goat's scrotum), has a unique taste and aroma unlike wine made from this rather ordinary grape elsewhere. Pale, light red wines come from the Ahr, fragrant riesling from Hessische Bergstrasse, and fruity, mild, easy-to-drink wines from the Mittelrhein. All of these wines have their fervent devotees.

In recent decades, German wines may have fallen out of fashion internationally, due to a move towards a taste for drier rather than sweeter styles. But taste is fickle and shifts in modern taste should have no bearing on wines that have historically satisfied for literally centuries. No wine lover should miss out on Germany's unique offerings made from grapes grown on the northernmost vineyards in Europe.

Elsewhere in Europe

France, Italy, Spain, Portugal and Germany may be the sources of classic European wines known and enjoyed around the world, but *Vitis vinifera* grows across the continent and wines are produced in a variety of countries. Indeed, the great legacy of the Romans means that vineyards that were planted more than 2,000 years ago continue to be cultivated today, even if in some cases the wines produced mainly serve to slake the thirst of local, regional and national wine lovers. In such circumstances, where demand exceeds limited supply, the only way to sample certain wines is to visit the country or area in question for yourself.

Swiss wines, for example, are rarely encountered outside Switzerland. Yet vineyards grace the shores of Lake Geneva and Neuchâtel, the warm area of the upper Rhône Valley known as the Valais, and Ticino, the Italian section of Switzerland. The wines produced, from light, zesty whites to full-bodied and flavourful reds, are varied and distinctive. They are not and never will be well known abroad, simply because there are not enough of them to go around. The Swiss are great wine drinkers and consume almost all of the wines that they produce themselves.

Austria is another alpine country that produces notable wines, albeit in relatively small quantities by global standards. The landscape of this landlocked country varies from the high Alps to the hot and steamy Pannonian Plain across which Roman legions once marched en route to Constantinople and the Eastern Empire. The vine is widely cultivated in Lower Austria leading up to the Czech border, in Styria, leading down to the border with Slovenia, in the Burgenland, especially around the Neusiedlersee, and even in Vienna itself. Wine styles range from fruity, dry wines made from the grüner veltliner grape in Lower Austria to spicy, rich whites from Styria. Burgenland, meanwhile, is the source of outstanding red wines made from indigenous grapes such as blaufrankisch, zweigelt and st laurent, as well as some of the most intriguing dessert wines in the world. These are made from grapes grown around the Neusiedlersee, where the conditions are just perfect for the regular and reliable formation of *Botrytis cinerea*.

Austria, of course, once lay at the heart of Europe, and oversaw a vast Austro-Hungarian empire. Indeed, wines from vineyards in what is now northeast Italy, Slovenia, Croatia and Hungary, as well as Austria itself, once graced the tables of emperors, kings and tsars. Hungary's famous Tokaji vineyards, located in the east of the country nearly on the borders of Slovakia and Ukraine, have long produced luscious and unique dessert wines that were particularly favoured by the tsars and by such royal personages as Louis xiv. During the decades when Eastern Europe was cut off from the West by the Iron Curtain, historic vineyards came under state control and the quality of the wines suffered. Today, tokaji is enjoying a renaissance, and the wines are better than ever, certainly worthy of their notable historic pedigree. Indeed, in Hungary as well as elsewhere, in countries such as Slovenia, Bulgaria and Romania, private enterprise is energizing once-moribund communist-state wine industries, and fine wines are emerging once more, utilizing both indigenous grapes and more familiar international varieties.

Greece, it might be assumed, as the homeland of European viticulture, should still have significant and deep vinous roots that were established millennia ago. Wine, we have noted, was central to life in the culture of ancient Greece, and indeed viticulture continued through the Middle Ages when Greece was part of the Byzantine Empire, with Constantinople the centre of a very active Mediterranean wine trade. However, when Byzantium fell and the Ottoman Turks occupied mainland Greece in the late fifteenth century, the Greek wine industry on a commercial scale virtually ceased. It is likely that the growing of grapes and the making of wine continued after a fashion, for private consumption, certainly on the islands as well as on the mainland. Though the Greeks managed to free themselves from the Ottoman Empire after the War of Independence waged in 1829, turmoil in the Balkans continued through the nineteenth and much of the twentieth century. The two world wars brought strife and occupation, and after the Second World War there was a bitter civil war in Greece. As a result, the modern Greek wine industry only really began after Greece joined what later became the European Union in 1981.

Throughout the years and centuries of occupation, the sturdy and prolific *Vitis vinifera* was never abandoned. Indeed, alongside other native plants such as the olive and caper bush, vines continued to grow on the mainland and islands alike. Today Greece is able to offer a range of indigenous grape varieties cultivated here (and virtually nowhere else on earth)

Historic wines such as tokaji, produced from grapes grown in eastern Hungary, once graced the tables of emperors and tsars. Today, after recovery from the decades under state control, this historic dessert wine is once again reaching former glories.

since time immemorial: little-known but characterful grapes such as assyrtiko, rhotitis, savatiano, aghiorghitiko, limnio, mandelaria and others. As Greece lies in a relatively hot zone for viticulture, modern technology, notably stainless-steel fermentation vessels with temperature control, allows for the production of modern wines with an individual character that comes from its ancient vinous patrimony.

Today Greece may almost be considered an emerging modern wine country. Yet among the things that still link the present-day country with its ancient past is a national taste for wines flavoured with pine resin. In antiquity, resin was used to line porous amphorae both to make such vessels watertight and to act as a preservative for the wine. The use of such an additive influenced the flavour and character of the wine. Today, white and rosé wines continue to be flavoured just so. This addition of pine resin lends a distinctive, sappy taste to the resulting retsina wines, loved by both locals and by tourists who have come to associate such resinated wines with the taste of summer holidays in Greece.

The Romans, we have seen, took the vine with them to virtually every land they conquered and colonized. Vineyards were planted extensively in Roman Britain some 2,000 years ago. If wine production ceased after the Romans left, Britain nonetheless maintained a long and illustrious history as a wine-drinking nation. Chaucer's pilgrims drank wine en route to Canterbury and Shakespeare's characters extolled the virtues of wine on numerous occasions.

In the last decades, England and Wales have emerged as serious wine-producing countries capable of producing wines with a character that distinctly reflects a unique cool-climate *terroir*. New vineyards are being planted at an exciting rate and the range of English and Welsh wines that is available is now greater than ever. The quantity will never be sufficient to

Pebblebed, an English rosé sparkling wine. Grapes have been cultivated in Britain since the Roman era, though the modern renaissance of English and Welsh wine is relatively recent.

slake a vast national thirst, yet, nonetheless, these wines now demand to be taken seriously. Outstanding sparkling wines are made from both hybrid grapes such as seyval blanc and *V. vinifera* varieties such as pinot noir and chardonnay. Such wines are now winning awards against the best in the world, even champagne. English still white and rosé wines can be attractive, capable of displaying a keen, fruity acidity and relatively low alcohol levels, in tune with today's tastes as consumers eschew heavier, more alcoholic examples from elsewhere in the world. Even red wines are being produced, notably from pinot noir, among other grape varieties.

As climate change brings warmer temperatures to Britain, it seems that the move to plant vineyards in England and Wales will only increase, while the resulting wines should continue to improve in quality and character.

4
A World of Wine

If *Vitis vinifera* originated in the Transcaucasus, it is fascinating to explore how over centuries and millennia it has spread to the far corners of the world.

The Americas

As every schoolchild knows, Christopher Columbus, with the backing of King Ferdinand and Queen Isabella of Castile, sailed across the Atlantic in 1492 to discover the Americas. The colonies were supposed to provide immeasurable wealth in raw materials as well as a ready market for export goods. Spain may have hoped that the New World would result in ready markets for its plentiful wines, but one problem was that it proved difficult for wine to survive the lengthy sea voyage across the tropics to arrive in a drinkable state.

By the time of the conquistadors, vines were being planted in the newly discovered lands that had been claimed on behalf of the kingdoms of Spain. Cortéz instructed all landowners in New Spain (modern Mexico) to plant vineyards and it was not long before this industry established deep roots on the new continents. Indeed, across the Americas, from the highlands of Mexico, across the southern coastal valleys of Peru, to the lower slopes of the Andes and even in areas totally unsuited to the cultivation of the grape vine, vineyards were planted, resulting in quantities of wines of apparently more or less drinkable quality.

Thus *V. vinifera*, a plant not originally native to the Americas, established itself. Today we may think of wines from Argentina, Chile, Uruguay or Mexico, let alone California's Napa or Sonoma Valleys, the damp, cool hills of Oregon and Washington, or the snow-covered wine slopes of Ontario, as arrivistes. But wine production and wine drinking have been an established part of the culture and way of living across the Americas for centuries.

North America

Long before the voyage of Christopher Columbus, Norse legends tell of Leif Ericson, who sailed across the Atlantic to establish the colony of Vinland, so named due to the profusion of wild vines in the new-found land. Were these vines grape-bearing? There is no mention of wines being made or of the fruit being consumed. However, the native grape vine does thrive across North America, and the prevailing species, *V. labrusca*, is indeed capable of producing a beverage that is potable.

The Europeans who came to North America in the sixteenth and seventeeth centuries brought *V. vinifera* with them, but the plant struggled to survive. It seems that winters were too bitterly cold and summers too hot, damp and humid, and the *Phylloxera* aphid, which in later centuries was to destroy the vineyards of Europe, ate its way happily through the newly planted vineyards. Yet viticulture stubbornly continued, most notably across the eastern seaboard in New York, New England, Pennsylvania, Virginia and into Southern states; in Canadian Ontario; in the Midwest along the Ohio River Valley and around the Great Lakes; and on the West Coast, most importantly in California, as well as in Oregon and Washington State, and up into British Columbia.

California's wine industry was started by Franciscan missionaries who first planted *V. vinifera* around 1770, following the Spanish instruction to all landowners to plant vineyards. Once Mexico threw off the shackles of Spain and became an independent nation, many of these missions were secularized and grape growing continued. After annexation by the United States, shortly followed by the Gold Rush, wine production expanded across the state from southern California to the wine hills north of San Francisco and beyond.

V. vinifera was always the preferred species in California. Certainly the state's fabled Mediterranean climate was more conducive to the cultivation of *vinifera* than elsewhere in the country. Furthemore, *vinifera* was preferred presumably because it was capable of producing wine that was – still is – infinitely more palatable than examples produced from native *V. labrusca*. By the late 1880s, some 300 varieties of *V. vinifera* were being cultivated in the Golden State by nearly 800 wineries. *Phylloxera* eventually arrived in the early twentieth century. An even greater setback was the introduction of Prohibition, which was in force from 1920 to 1933. With the Second World War following soon after, it was decades before the Californian wine industry recovered.

Today, California remains the largest source of American wine by far; indeed, the state itself is one of the largest producers of wine in the world. Although as recently as the 1970s and '80s, much of what was produced in California was fairly indifferent, including vast quantities of jug wines and bottles sold with ersatz generic European names – 'burgundy', 'port', 'chablis' and the like – California today is undoubtedly the source of some of the greatest wines in the world. Californian wine can be both handcrafted in boutique wineries or mass-produced in large ones, mainly from familiar European grape varieties such as cabernet sauvignon, merlot, syrah and pinot noir for reds, and chardonnay, sauvignon blanc and chenin blanc for whites. Zinfandel, related (as DNA evidence indicates) to an obscure grape variety from Slovenia's Dalmatian coast, is a unique Californian speciality. Other notable varieties planted with some considerable success include sangiovese and barbera (of Tuscan and Piedmontese fame respectively), pinot gris (or grigio), riesling, gewürztraminer, sémillon and viognier.

Meanwhile, the Pacific Northwest states of Oregon and Washington have emerged as outstanding sources of wines produced from select *V. vinifera* grapes. Oregon's settled and bucolic Willamette Valley may contrast with Washington's rugged, remote and sometimes inhospitable Columbia and Yakima Valleys. Both are sources of harmonious wines that benefit from a cool climate, with a considerable variation between day- and night-time temperatures, and a long growing season. Oregon is most famous for its fine, burgundy-like pinot noirs, while in Washington State merlot and cabernet sauvignon grow well. Aromatic grapes such as riesling and sauvignon blanc can result in wines combining scent and elegance.

If America's wine industry originally started on the other side of the country, the East Coast is yet to catch up with the West in terms of quality. The problem has always been that *V. vinifera* found it harder to take root there. Not only is the climate less beneficial, with long, severe winters and hellishly hot, humid summers, but also *Phylloxera* has historically been harder to eradicate, repeatedly destroying vineyards that were

Napa Valley vineyard. California's wine industry dates back to the 18th century, when vineyards were planted by Franciscan missionaries.

Cool-climate vineyards in Pacific Northwest states such as Washington and Oregon are outstanding sources of both red wines from pinor noir, merlot and cabernet sauvignon grapes and white wines from aromatic grape varieties such as riesling and sauvignon blanc.

on the verge of becoming established. However, hybrid varieties produced from cross-breeding European plants with native ones were not only hearty enough to be able to withstand the harsh northeast winters as well as the ravages of *Phylloxera*, but they were also capable of producing wines with much more acceptable flavour profiles than the heavy, 'foxy' wines made entirely from the native *V. labrusca*.

New York State has produced wine commercially since at least 1860. Today vineyards are established throughout the state, from Long Island to Lake Erie, and there are more than 200 wineries. Some of the best wines come from vineyards planted above the beautiful Finger Lakes. Hybrid grapes include seyval blanc, aurora, cayuga and vidal blanc. *Vinifera* varieties that are successful include chardonnay, riesling, gewürztraminer and sauvignon blanc. The ubiquitous *V. labrusca* concord is widely planted and used not only to make a wine of sorts but also table grapes, grape juice and grape jelly.

While vines are cultivated in isolated areas up and down the East Coast, Virginia can claim historic vineyards dating back to the seventeenth and eighteenth centuries. Thomas Jefferson, after all, was an avid winegrower and there were vineyards at Monticello. 'We could, in the United States, make as great a variety of wines as are made in Europe, not exactly the same kinds, but doubtless as good', claimed the third president of the United States.

Though by the 1960s the Virginian wine industry had almost completely died out, recent decades have seen a revival and the results are more than encouraging, with some excellent examples of Virginia wines made from classic European grape varieties such as chardonnay, riesling, sauvignon blanc, merlot and cabernet sauvignon. The state now has no less than six American Viticultural Areas (AVAs) with monticello AVA named in tribute to Jefferson. In fact, the Monticello Wine Trail leads to some 24 boutique wineries as well as passing by the homes of three former US presidents (Madison and Monroe in addition to Jefferson).

Elsewhere, Ohio can boast a well-established (if never overly distinguished) wine industry, while there are also notable vineyards in states such as Idaho, Texas, New Mexico, Missouri, Arkansas and elsewhere.

In Canada, outstanding wines are being produced in Ontario; there is also wine production in Nova Scotia and Quebec, as well as to the far west in British Columbia. It seems the Canadians managed to steal a march on their American neighbours to the south by establishing vineyards during the era of Prohibition, and the Canadian industry has continued to produce wines ever since.

Ontario's climate can create exemplary results. The extremely dry, cold weather of the Ontario winters means that grapes can be left on the vine to reach their maximum ripeness.

Ice wine is produced from grapes that are left on the vine so late that they actually freeze. Ontario is the source of some of the world's best examples.

Once freezing conditions arrive, the grapes can be carefully harvested and pressed immediately, before the ice within the grapes thaws. This sugar-rich, concentrated grape juice can be the source of magnificent, luscious perfumed dessert ice wines that are simply fabulous – and truly world-class.

Central and South America

Like the Romans who took the vine with them to the lands they conquered, the European conquistadors who came to Mexico, Central America and South America brought *V. vinifera* with them. After the conquistadors came the missionaries, who landed on a new continent to save the souls of the natives they encountered. The need for wine to celebrate the Eucharist would have been pressing and thus many of the first vineyards planted successfully in the New World may have had ecclesiastic origins. The mission wines of California (at that time a part of New Spain), as well as wines produced by Jesuit missionaries in Peru from the seventeenth century, are evidence of this. Yet, as early as the mid-sixteenth century, wine was already more than a beverage reserved just for the Church: it had become an indispensable element of daily life, especially for those Europeans who had come over to settle on a new continent to carve out a new life and fortune for themselves.

Indeed, wine was a beverage linked to the old country that was health-giving – and often better and safer to drink than the local water. But transporting wines from Spain or Portugal to the Americas by sea was not easy – the wooden casks of liquid wine would have taken up considerable space in the holds of ships, and the heat and churning movement, followed by transport overland sometimes hundreds and thousands of miles, would have meant that the wines were often spoiled and undrinkable on arrival at their destination. Planting vineyards to produce home-grown wines was the obvious answer, provided that *V. vinifera* could withstand a new and sometimes hostile environment.

Though it may have been a requirement for all new landowners in New Spain to plant vineyards, Mexico never established a vibrant wine culture. Was this because the indigenous natives and the mestizo population that subsequently followed preferred the home-grown taste of pulque, a pre-Columbian alcoholic beverage made from the fermented sap of the maguey cactus? Pulque was considered sacred and it is probable that it was originally reserved for priests, sacrificial victims and rulers. The drink became more widely enjoyed after the Spanish conquest, and it was no doubt the Spaniards who introduced distillation to the Americas. By fermenting and then distilling a mash made from the maguey, they created mezcal, a potent highly alcoholic spirit not dissimilar to tequila. These potent, sometimes hallucinogenic drinks became widely popular. Could this be why even today the production of distilled grape brandy is more popular in Mexico than the production of table wines?

Of course the excessive heat of Mexico, combined with tropical or near-tropical latitudes across much of the country, were never overly conducive to the production of quality wines from *V. vinifera*. It is no surprise, then, that some of the best results come from the cool-climate vineyards of South America. Not only was climate and geography a factor in the success of wines in the Americas, but historical settlements from Europe also had a bearing on the development of the wine industry.

Argentina's most important wine region, the Mendoza Valley, for example, has had land under vines from as long ago

V. vinifera has been cultivated in Argentina's Mendoza at the foot of the Andes since as long ago as 1557, when Jesuit missionaries first planted the grape vine. In subsequent centuries, settlers from Europe brought their own grape-growing traditions and winemaking skills.

as 1557, originally cultivated by the Jesuit missionaries who settled there. Indeed, winegrowing on a commercial scale was in place as early as the late sixteenth century. After Argentina gained independence from Spain in the 1820s, waves of settlers from Europe came, bringing with them grape-growing traditions, vine cuttings, winemaking skills and knowledge from their homes in France, Spain and Italy. They also brought with them a culture of wine drinking: by the 1960s Argentina could boast the third highest per capita wine consumption in the world. Today consumption has declined; the vines to produce the rough table wines that used to make up the bulk of production have been grubbed up, and the country is now the source of both sound everyday as well as high-quality wines from *V. vinifera* grapes grown on the foothills of the Andes. Malbec, originally a French variety, has transplanted particularly well to the other side of the world and today makes Argentina's most distinctive red wine.

Across the other side of this impressive and high mountain range, vineyards in Chile were also planted historically as early as the mid-sixteenth century, notably on the fertile lands outside and around Santiago, the country's capital. As elsewhere on the continent, conquistadors, settlers and missionaries are all credited with bringing viticulture to the country. Indeed some vineyards around Santiago can claim over 400 years of continuous wine production. When the vineyards of France were devastated by *Phylloxera*, French winegrowers came to Chile to seek new livelihoods. The industry grew in the nineteenth and twentieth centuries and today Chile is the source of a range of outstanding wines made primarily from international varieties of *V. vinifera*, including sauvignon blanc, merlot, cabernet sauvignon, syrah and pinot noir.

Elsewhere in South America, the vine was brought to Brazil by Portuguese settlers, though the hot, humid climate of much of the country made it difficult for *V. vinifera* to establish itself. Indeed, native American grape varieties were cultivated

Elquí Valley, Chile. Vineyards in Chile can claim over 400 years of continuous production. The country received a further boost when winemakers came here from France at the end of the 19th century after their vineyards had been devastated by *Phylloxera*.

more easily and today table grapes remain more important to the Brazilian economy than wine grapes. The best wines come from the south of the country towards the border with Uruguay and Argentina.

In terms of volume, Uruguay may rank behind Brazil, but vineyards planted originally by Basque and Italian settlers are capable of producing noteworthy wines. The bulk of the production is either drunk within the country, or sold across the border to the thirsty Brazilians.

Australia

The Australian continent, inhabited for possibly 40,000 years or more by its indigenous population, was discovered by Dutch explorers in 1606 and claimed by the British in 1770, at which time it became a penal colony. Vine cuttings were brought to New South Wales in 1782, and by 1820, commercial viticulture was established with vineyards planted exclusively with *V. vinifera* vines imported from Europe, since the continent lacked any native varieties of its own.

European immigrants brought not only vines with them but also wine traditions and culture: from Italy, Germany, Switzerland, France, the Balkans and elsewhere. *V. vinifera*, it seems, thrived pretty well on this southern hemisphere continent, from the Hunter Valley north of Sydney in New South Wales across to the Clare, Eden and Barossa Valleys of South Australia; and from the Yarra Valley and Mornington Peninsula of Victoria and the Margaret River and Swan Valley of Western Australia to the cool-climate vineyards of Tasmania.

Well-cultivated fruit grown in propitious microclimates suited to the cultivation of *V. vinifera,* allied with skilful winemaking in tune with European taste, yielded considerable results.

By the end of the nineteenth century, Australian wines were already winning awards and accolades against even the best that France could offer (to the not inconsiderable chagrin of the French).

More vineyards were planted, often in warmer regions, and the style of wine moved over towards the production of sweet and fortified wine, which were extremely popular with the British. Indeed, between 1927 and 1939, Australia exported more wine to its old mother country than did France.

Australia today has a mature wine industry that is the source of both plentiful and affordable everyday wines as well as premium wines of the highest quality. While there is considerable regional variety between the wines produced throughout this vast country, the quality of fruit allied with the most modern winemaking technologies means that Australia is consistently able to produce a range of approachable and distinctive wines marketed by both brand and grape variety that find favour with consumers around the world.

Indeed, it would not be going too far to say that if the classic wines of France have historically served as benchmark models for wines produced elsewhere in the world, then Australia has pointed the way with the production of its own New World classics. I'm thinking of iconic wines such as Penfold's Grange (a wine that is as impressive – and as expensive – as those of Bordeaux's top châteaux) as well as other heavyweight shiraz and cabernet reds from the Barossa Valley, McLaren Vale and Hunter Valley; more elegant and European-style reds from pinot noir and cabernet sauvignon from the Margaret and Swan Valleys of Western Australia; oak-matured chardonnays and sémillons from the Yarra and Hunter Valleys and the Mornington Peninsula; racy, dry riesling from the Clare and Eden Valleys; pungent yet not overblown New World sauvignon blancs from the Margaret River and Adelaide

South Australia's Barossa Valley is one of the country's best wine regions, most notable for its powerful and silky red wines produced from shiraz and cabernet sauvignon grapes.

Hills; and outstanding sparkling wines from Tasmania. The list goes on.

What is perhaps most refreshing about Australia's wine industry is that it is not staitjacketed by tradition. New (or at least relatively new to Australia) grape varieties are being experimented with, including whites such as savagnin, albariño, verdelho, vermentino and reds such as tempranillo, sangiovese and nebbiolo. The results are never less than fascinating. Australia continues to lead in terms of its willingness to embrace modern wine technology, too. What would be innovative elsewhere is now standard here: for example, night and mechanical

harvesting; the use of specialist yeasts; maturation using oak planks or chips to impart flavour; and closure by Stelvin or screw-cap (it is, in fact, difficult to find an Australian wine that is not screw-cap). At the end of the day, good – and great – wine comes from quality fruit allied with good winemaking techniques, driven by passionate individuals whose aim is to produce the very best. Australia has an abundance of all of these features.

New Zealand

As elsewhere in the world, it was probably well-intentioned missionaries who first brought the European grape vine to

New Zealand, sometime in the early part of the nineteenth century. It is fortuitous that the country's first British resident, James Busby, was also a keen viticulturist who established a vineyard as early as 1836 and attempted to produce wine on his land at Waitangi. The industry, however, never really took off as the mainly British settlers did not bring with them a wine-drinking culture, preferring instead to drink beer. When *Phylloxera* devastated the islands' vineyards the problem was solved not, as elsewhere, by grafting American rootstock onto *V. vinifera*, but by planting American and hybrid grape varieties instead. Furthermore, restrictions on the sale of alcohol were another barrier to the creation of a national wine industry.

The modern wine industry in New Zealand, now established globally, only dates back to as recently as the 1960s and '70s. At that time, hybrid vines were grubbed up and a new generation of winegrowers dedicated themselves to the production of high-quality grapes that were able to thrive in a cooler microclimate.

Indeed the world was to discover that New Zealand, never previously considered a serious wine-producing country, possessed a *terroir* that is particularly well suited to the production of finely scented wines from aromatic grape varieties such as sauvignon blanc. The notoriously fickle and difficult to grow pinot noir was also, it was discovered, capable of producing outstanding results: wines that have a subtlety and character that is considered almost burgundian.

Vineyards are established today on both the North Island (notably Auckland, Hawke's Bay and Wellington) and the South Island, with Marlborough the premier wine zone. While New Zealand sauvignon blanc has come to be regarded as a benchmark in its own right, producing wines that have a unique and fine character that is different to yet of equal calibre to the famous French wines sancerre and pouilly-fumé, the country's

Vineyards on Waiheke Island, New Zealand. While wine grapes have been cultivated in New Zealand since the early part of the 19th century, it is only in recent decades that the country has emerged as an exciting source of outstanding wines from aromatic varieties such as sauvignon blanc and silky and Burgundian-like reds from pinot noir.

varied wine country has proved itself a propitious habitat for the cultivation of a range of varietals, including chardonnay, riesling, sémillon and pinot gris for whites and cabernet sauvignon, merlot and syrah for reds, in addition to pinot noir.

Today, New Zealand's still young and evolving wine industry is dynamic. It has established itself as a source of world-class wines that simply could not come from anywhere else. Indeed, New Zealand is an ongoing example of how the world of quality wine has expanded within a relatively short period of time.

South Africa

It is easy to view the so-called New World countries as johnny-come-latelies to the world of fine wine. Far from it: vineyards have been established on South Africa's Cape since the mid-seventeenth century, cultivated with cuttings of *V. vinifera* brought from France and elsewhere. Wines from Constantia, produced on estates established in the seventeenth century, are historic wines that in their day were considered a match for the greatest from France or Germany. Its concentrated muscat dessert wines were particularly appreciated and enjoyed by European aristocracy and royalty.

By the early part of the twentieth century, the country had a wine glut, with more produced than could be sold or consumed. A cooperative was formed – the Koöperatieve Wijnbouwers Vereniging van Zuid-Afrika Bpkt (KWV) – and its solution was to encourage the production of wines for distillation into grape brandy and for the production of fortified dessert wines.

During the years of apartheid, South Africa was isolated through the boycotting of its products. It was only in the late 1980s and '90s that the wine industry began to recover and experience something of a renaissance. Vineyards were replanted with premium grape varieties such as shiraz, cabernet sauvignon, chenin blanc and sauvignon blanc. Meanwhile, KWV gave way to private estates, and a healthy export market has been established.

Today South Africa is producing a range of outstanding and exciting varietal wines of real class and quality. Its wine country, primarily in the Western Cape, is well developed for tourism and is among the most welcoming in the world.

Asia Minor, the Middle East
and North Africa

The origins of winemaking lie somewhere deep in the Trans-caucasus, in the lands located between the Black Sea and the Caspian Sea. It was here that Neolithic man mastered the domestication of *V. vinifera*, planted vineyards and made the world's first wine. Archaeological evidence demonstrates a high degree of sophistication, with irrigation canals, underground wine cellars, the production of clay vessels for fermentation and wine storage, and beautifully decorated wine cups for the enjoyment of the fruits of early man's labours.

Today grapes continue to be grown across Azerbaijan and Armenia on a relatively small commercial scale, resulting in a range of wines that are enjoyed and sought after, particularly

It is fitting that in the part of the world where wine most likely originated, today in Georgia wines are still fermented in terracotta jars, sometimes buried underground, as they have been for literally thousands of years.

The Holy Land has long been a propitious habitat for the vine. Today in modern Israel vineyards are planted and wines produced, both for everyday consumption and for use in the Kiddush ceremony.

by the Russians. Georgia's wine industry is much more fully developed. There is a centuries-old culture of wine drinking in this independent republic that was formerly a part of the Soviet Union. Under the Soviets, Georgia supplied vast quantities of wine to slake the thirst of the Russian market. That old state industry is no more. There has been considerable private investment, however, and a strong historic wine culture remains. It is estimated that some 500 indigenous grape varieties are still cultivated here. On a small scale, some wines are still produced traditionally as they have been for centuries, making no concession to international taste. Some white wines, for example, are still fermented in clay amphorae, resulting in old-style oxidized wine that offer something of the flavour of the types of wine that our ancestors once drank.

From the Transcaucasus, the vine travelled to the Levant and the Mediterranean. Indeed the vine was widely planted in the Holy Land as noted in the Bible. If one believes that Noah was the first to make wine, then it would seem that the grape vine has been cultivated in these lands from the earliest days of creation. What is beyond doubt is that in the lands that form modern Israel as well as in neighbouring Lebanon, grapes have flourished in near-ideal conditions and wines have been made continuously literally for millennia.

Wine is of course of vital importance to Jewish culture and religion. On the Sabbath, the Kiddush is recited over sacramental wines, and thus wine is an integrated part of Jewish life. By no means all of Israel's wine industry is dedicated to the production of kosher wines. Increasingly, vineyards planted at higher altitudes in areas such as Galilee with international grape varieties including cabernet sauvignon, merlot, sauvignon blanc and chardonnay, are demonstrating that fine table wines can be produced here.

Lebanon is another ancient wine-producing country with a long and notable history. The Phoenicians, those ancient seafaring merchants who carried the vine with them across the Mediterranean, came from what is now the modern state of Lebanon. The Greeks and Romans appreciated the wines of Canaan and the Bekaa Valley. Even under the Ottoman Empire, when winemaking was forbidden, Christians were given special dispensation to produce wine 'for religious purposes'.

After the First World War, Lebanon was mandated to France, finally gaining independence in 1943. The French brought prosperity and a sophisticated and cosmopolitan style to Beirut, the capital city, including a thriving wine-drinking culture. Vineyards in the Bekaa Valley that had been cultivated for millennia were able to supply wines not just for home consumption but even for export. After independence and during

Vineyards at Huadong Chateau, Qingdao. China, not currently known as a major wine-producing country, has seen considerable increases in the plantation of vineyards since the 1980s. Today it is the source of high-quality wines, mainly enjoyed within the country, which will almost certainly become known internationally in the years to come.

the years of the country's civil war, and through ongoing conflicts with Israel, French-influenced wine estates, notably Château Musar, have continued to battle against adversity, producing wines of the highest quality from classic grape varieties in one of the world's oldest continuous vineyards.

If the French inspired winemakers in the Lebanon, Gallic influence in North Africa had an even greater impact on the local wine industries. While vines had grown across North Africa in the classical era, it was in the nineteenth century that

viticulture was revived across the north of the continent, partly in response to the ravages of *Phylloxera*. Vineyards were planted in Algeria, a former French colony, and the country became a plentiful source of wines that were high in alcohol and colour. Such wines consequently found their way into the blending vats to bolster insipid vintages from the mother country. Indeed, even exalted wines such as burgundy apparently benefited from the boost of colour and alcohol that such hot-country wines could give – this of course in an era when the controls over such practices were considerably more lax than they are today. However, Algeria's wine industry suffered something of a collapse after independence in 1962 and has never fully recovered.

Morocco, like Algeria, is another former French colony that once had a significant wine industry, most notably in the 1950s and '60s. Independence saw the loss of its most important market, and the area under vines declined dramatically. Both countries benefit from classification systems modelled on the French *appellation d'origine contrôlée*.

Asia

The vast continent of Asia has never been considered a serious source of wines produced from *V. vinifera*. However, in the very near future this may well change. As Asian countries have emerged as economic powerhouses, a new generation of wine drinkers has similarly appeared, enthusiastic consumers eager to learn, to taste, to drink and to buy. Asian countries such as China, Japan, South Korea, Indonesia, Thailand, Vietnam, Taiwan and India are all important emerging markets for winemakers around the world.

China, the world's most populous country, is estimated to become the biggest market for wine within just a few decades as prosperity brings a desire for Western consumer products. To meet the demand, vineyards have been planted since the 1980s and it is probable that the country will one day soon become a global force in wine production, capable of producing both volume as well as wines of quality. Large established brands include Dynasty (a joint venture with Rémy Martin) and the Great Wall Wine Company. The latter produces some 100 different types of wine, much of which is now consumed within the domestic market. As the Chinese economy expands and Western lifestyle products continue to be seen as status symbols, it is likely that both wine consumption and production will continue to grow at an exponential pace and new names will emerge that will soon expand into export markets.

India is another country that has a fast-emerging wine-drinking populace. Here too vineyards are being planted to meet increasing demand. Table wines produced from *V. vinifera* grapes such as chardonnay, cabernet sauvignon and merlot are appreciated by a new generation of middle-class Indian wine drinkers. Grover Vineyards, based in Bangalore, is a leading company whose wines are finding success in both domestic and export markets, while Indage, Sula, Sankalp and Renaissance are all up-and-coming companies. Indian wines, including a limited but increasing amount of sparkling wines, are also finding further success enjoyed in Indian restaurants around the world.

Due to modern winemaking techniques, most notably fermentation in temperature-controlled stainless-steel vessels, drinkable wines can be produced from grapes grown in countries that previously would have been considered too hot. It is probable that in years and decades to come, even more new countries will emerge as serious producers of wine.

5
From Grape to Glass

The character as well as the quality of wine is determined by the quality of the grapes used to produce it, with myriad factors coming into play: grape variety, *terroir*, yield, variations in weather and precipitation leading up to the moment of harvest, and crucial decisions made in the winemaking process throughout the year. All of these factors may determine whether a wine is merely drinkable or wholly exceptional.

The technological process of transforming grapes into an alcoholic beverage capable of being conserved is fundamental to the creation of this unique agricultural product. The transformation of grape to wine is on one level remarkably basic, virtually unchanged for centuries; on another, it is a complex demonstration of man's incredible ingenuity and creativity.

Indeed, the biggest single determinant of style as well as quality, after the grape variety itself, is the human element, the decisions taken in the vineyard and the wine cellar to process and transform fresh grapes into wine.

The Technology of Winemaking

At the most basic level, wine can be produced in much the same way as it has always been. Grapes are harvested by hand and transported to a winemaking facility where they are crushed and added to a fermentation receptacle. The natural yeasts present on the skins begin to feed on the grape sugars and this provokes fermentation, which continues until either the supply of sugars is exhausted or alcohol reaches a level high enough to kill off the yeast (usually around 15 or 16 per cent).

Our ancient Neolithic ancestors made wines following this basic process. The human foot, it was probably discovered at an early stage, was the perfect tool with which to crush grapes gently yet effectively. Though modern technology is widely available today, this process is still used in some parts of the wine world even now, notably in the port quintas of Portugal's Upper Douro, where the annual ritual of men and women crushing the grapes with their bare feet to the rhythmic beat of folk music is very much alive. This is not mere picturesque folklore, either: using the foot, it turns out, is still one of the best ways to release juice, as well as to crush the grape skins gently in order to facilitate the maximum extraction of colour and flavour elements without damaging the grape pips, which would contribute bitter or unpleasant flavours.

The discovery of a means to make wine systematically and dependably dates back to the Neolithic period, a time that coincided with technological advances that impacted not just on the development of wine but on the history and evolution of civilization itself. The ability to make earthenware vessels hardened with fire and thus capable of holding liquids in quantity was one such significant technological achievement that allowed for the development of winemaking. Such vessels were used for fermentation as well as for the storage and transport of wines throughout the ancient world. It is interesting to note that in the Transcaucasus, near where wine possibly originated, notably in Georgia, wines are still fermented in earthenware jars buried underground, following a process that has changed little over the past 8,000 years.

From the earliest era, the ancients developed ingenious winemaking techniques. Egyptian hieroglyphics depict a simple but effective mechanical means of squeezing or pressing grapes: the grape residue or pomace was placed in a bag held up between two poles, and the poles were twisted around in order to squeeze out the juice, to be captured in jars below. Once the wines had finished fermentation, other glyphs illustrate servants sealing the wine jars with clay to keep out oxygen and so allow the wines to be conserved for lengthy periods.

We have already noted that Etruscan cellars still in use in wine towns such as Orvieto demonstrate an intricate and well-thought-out winemaking system utilizing the natural cool underground temperature. Consider how today modern wine producers go to the greatest expense, utilizing temperature-controlled stainless-steel fermentation vats in an attempt to mirror these same age-old, natural, temperature-controlled conditions.

Other technological developments were fundamental to the evolution of wine. For example, the Romans came to use the wooden barrel in place of the amphora as a receptacle for wine when it is was introduced from Gaul sometime in the third century AD. The art of creating a watertight receptacle from wooden staves shaped and bent by the application of fire had probably been perfected some centuries earlier. As receptacles for wine, barrels were cheaper and more robust than amphorae; they could be repaired if broken; and they were easier to transport. Indeed, wooden barrels came to be used not only for storage and transport of wine but for fermentation, with large barrels and vats constructed in a similar fashion by skilled coopers.

If wooden barrels were primarily utilized as receptacles for storage and transport, as well as fermentation vessels, one consequence was that the porosity of wooden barrels allowed micro-oxygenation to take place, allowing the wine contained within to mature and evolve with age. A further benefit was that flavours and aromas that wood, especially new oak, imparted to the wine, though extraneous to the flavours and aroma of the grape itself, were considered pleasing. Indeed, the silky, vanilla tones that derive from new French oak have come to be considered an essential component of the wine itself. For this reason, today even wines fermented in stainless steel may have oak flavourings imparted to them, by maturation in new oak barrels as well as from oak chips suspended in wine like giant tea bags, or through the use of replaceable wooden staves slotted into the stainless-steel vessels.

The manufacture of the glass bottle was another invention that played an important role in the history of wine. The amphora and the barrel were receptacles for holding large quantities of wine, but neither could be tapped easily for service at the table. Not only were such vessels inconveniently large, but the wine contained within would also, unless consumed very rapidly, oxidize quickly, turn to vinegar and consequently spoil.

Though the Romans had perfected the art of blowing glass bottles and probably used them for the storage and service of wine (there is a Roman glass bottle still containing ancient wine in a museum in Speyer, Germany), usually Roman wines were transferred from amphorae into decorative ceramic wine vessels. Throughout Europe, from the Middle Ages through the Renaissance, pottery and stoneware jugs continued to be used to serve wines until as late as the sixteenth century, when the Venetians perfected the art of glass-making and began to manufacture glass decanters.

Hand-blown bottles, however, did not begin to be manufactured commercially before the seventeenth century. Each bottle had to be individually blown, so they came in a variety of shapes and sizes, with no uniform volume capacity. Bottles were often closed with glass stoppers that were ground to fit the shape of each bottle's individual neck. Such stoppers continued to be used, like the glass stoppers in a decanter, well into the nineteenth century. However, the discovery (or rediscovery) of natural cork gradually resulted in the most efficient – as well as cost-effective – means of closing a bottle.

The evolution of wine has been linked to advances in technology, from the mastery of creating pottery fermentation and storage vessels, watertight barrels and casks, to the manufacturing of glass bottles. This Roman two-handled wine bottle dates from AD 70–150.

The creation of sparkling wines was made possible once bottles could be manufactured that were consistently able to withstand the considerable internal pressure without breaking. The bottles were originally sealed with corks that were tied down with string in order to keep them in the bottle and thus trap the bubbles within the wine.

The transition to putting wines in bottles sealed with corks was therefore an important moment in the evolution of wine. Though it was long known that the best wines had the capacity to improve with age, prior to this time, ageing had been carried out in large vessels – either amphorae or wooden casks or barrels. Laying down bottles of wine sealed with corks allowed for bottle ageing whereby fine wines such as vintage port, bordeaux and burgundy, vinified with lengthy extract and so rich in tannin and other preservatives, could slowly improve through maturation in the bottle over a period of years (in some cases, centuries). In the case of champagne, the use of the bottle and the cork (tied down with string or held down with a wire cage) allowed for the perfection of secondary fermentation in the bottle, resulting in the greatest sparkling wine in the world.

In these instances, technological advances positively resulted in the creation or evolution of wine types and styles, as well as leading to improvements in quality.

Indeed, it is only in the most recent decades that new technologies have replaced some of these traditional means of production, such as the introduction of temperature-controlled stainless-steel fermentation vessels (in place of wooden, concrete or earthenware fermentation vessels), the use of alternative means of bottle closure such as Stelvin (screw-cap) or plastic stoppers, and even the use of containers other than the bottle, such as the winebox or the paper bottle.

Louis Pasteur

If our ancestors understood many of the fundamentals of winemaking, the production of modern wine only became a true science following the researches of Louis Pasteur. Through his groundbreaking investigations into fermentation carried out in the mid-nineteenth century, Pasteur identified micro-organisms involved in the process of transforming alcohol into sugar and proved the need to keep harmful micro-bacteria at bay. Early man had understood the need to keep wine from oxidizing and thus turning into vinegar, so means were adapted to achieve this through careful hygiene and storage in airtight receptacles. Yet even up to Pasteur's time, the regular souring of wine (as well as beer and milk) was a serious problem that had real economic ramifications. It was only when Pasteur, a chemist and biologist, undertook his precise and scientific experiments that the chemical and biological fundamentals of fermentation came to be more fully understood. Through his researches, Pasteur helped to make the mysteries of wine more understandable and laid down scientific procedures that remain the cornerstone of modern winemaking today.

Modern Winemaking

How then are wines produced today? As in the past, the making of wine begins in the vineyard. Clearly, care and attention in the vineyard through all phases of the annual cycle are required in order to result in fruit with sufficient sugar, balanced acidity and concentration of flavour to result in good wine. Grape variety or varieties; terrain, microclimate and *terroir*; particular climatic conditions at precise and critical moments throughout the year; training methods; treatments utilized to eradicate pests as well as reduce disease; pruning and green pruning to reach the desired yields; and decisions regarding the ripeness of the grapes and the optimum moment to harvest are among the many vineyard determinants of quality and character.

Once harvested, yet more factors and decisions impact on the finished wine. There are, however, broad blueprints for the production of the main types and styles of modern wine: white, rosé, red, sparkling, dessert and fortified wines.

On arrival from the vineyard at the winemaking facility, and regardless of the style of wine to be made, the first step, usually, is to pass the grapes through a destemmer-crusher, a machine that separates the stems from the berries and lightly crushes them to release the juice (the exception is whole-grape fermentation for wines such as beaujolais nouveau).

White Wines

Modern white wines are fermented from the must or juice that is released when the grapes are crushed. Unlike red wines, they are not usually fermented in contact with the grape skins (though sometimes the juice is left to macerate on the skins for a brief period to extract greater flavour and character). The crushed grapes are next pressed – in modern wineries usually in a horizontal press that gently releases the juice without extracting coarse or harsh flavours or tannin from the skins or grape pips. Any solid matter is removed from the pure grape must or juice, which is then transferred to a fermentation vessel. This may be made out of stainless steel, concrete, fibreglass or wood. Cultivated yeasts may be added to begin the fermentation, or else wild yeasts that are present on the grapes or in the winery may be deemed sufficient, indeed preferable, to get fermentation going. Stainless-steel is often preferred today in modern wineries because it is easy to clean and also because it facilitates temperature-controlled fermentation. Temperature control during fermentation is very important particularly for the production of white wines: low

One of the most significant advances in technology in recent decades has been the widespread implementation of temperature-controlled stainless-steel fermentation vats. These allow wines to be produced even in hot climates, and lend winemakers more precise control over myriad and sometimes haphazard variables.

temperatures can result in very clean white wines that maintain fruit, fragrance and freshness above all.

Other fermentation vessels may be concrete, large wooden casks or fibreglass. Some white wines are barrel-fermented, that is, the grape must is added to small 225-litre oak barrels to ferment and afterwards to age on the lees, the residue left over after fermentation. For those wines with sufficient structure and concentration, barrel-fermentation can result in fuller, richer flavours and character, as well as the mellow, vanilla tones that come from new oak.

Red Wines

The grapes for red wines, by contrast, after destemming and crushing, are usually pumped skins and all into the fermentation vessel or vat. The skins, pips and other solid matter are vital for imparting colour to red wine, as well as tannin and other elements that enable such wines to be conserved and so improve and develop with age. The mass of skins naturally sits at the top of the fermentation vat, and this must be kept wine-drenched, often by pumping grape must from the bottom of the vat back up to the top to percolate through it, thus extracting more colour, tannin and flavouring elements. This process of pumping over may need to be done as often as three times a day during the primary fermentation.

Once the winemaker has deemed that fermentation is complete and the wine has steeped for a sufficiently long period on the skins, the wine is run off from the skins, and the resulting solid residue is then put through a press. The press wine is naturally harsher and richer in tannin than the wine that has fermented in the tank or vat, and this is added judiciously to the final blend to provide body and structure.

Afterwards, the solid mass of grape skins is sent off to the distillery to be transformed into highly potent alcoholic distillations such as marc and grappa.

For most red wines, some time after the first or tumultuous fermentation has been completed, a further secondary fermentation is usually allowed to take place. This is the malolactic fermentation, a bacterial fermentation that converts harsher malic acid into softer lactic acid. White wines can also undergo this natural process, though those wines that seek to preserve a crisp freshness might forgo the malolactic fermentation in order to maintain the refreshing green-apple flavours and aromas that come from malic acid.

Simple red wines destined to be drunk while young and fresh are racked, that is, taken off the lees or sediment to a clean vessel, and they may continue to be stored in an inert stainless-steel, or other, vat. Before bottling, the wine must be fined, a process that causes solid matters to precipitate, and

Tradition in winemaking still lives on in historic and classic wine regions such as Burgundy. Here silky red burgundies age in oak barrels, a process that lends more complex flavours and structure to those wines that are able to support them.

possibly filtered to remove any further substances or solid particles prior to bottling.

More serious reds undergo further ageing in wooden barrels, either in large traditional old wooden casks (which do not normally impart wood flavours), or in smaller new or nearly new barrels made with either French or American oak. The provenance of the oak has an impact on flavour and character. American oak imparts a completely different character from French oak, and even oak from different forests, for example Vosges, Limousin, Tronçais, Nevers or Allier, will display a distinctive character. Even the degree to which the barrels have been toasted when they are constructed (fire helps to bend the staves) can be important to the character that the barrels impart to the finished wine. Time spent in wood can vary from a brief period of a month or two just to polish off any rough edges, to a lengthy sojourn of upwards of two or three years, or even longer.

The above outlines the process of red wine-making at its most basic. There are numerous variations. Carbonic maceration, for example, is a process of whole-grape fermentation whereby grapes are not first crushed but put whole into a sealed fermentation tank. This process yields wines that are particularly fresh and fruity and is used to make wines destined to be drunk very young.

Rosé Wines

Rosé wines have grown in popularity in recent times. They can vary in colour from the palest pink to a quite full colour that almost borders on red. The flesh of most wine grapes is pale, not coloured. The colour in wine comes from the contact of the juice with the skins, a process that extracts not only hue but also tannin and other flavouring elements. The best rosé wines are made by allowing the crushed and pressed grapes to have just sufficient maceration on the skins to leech out the desired hue. Once this is reached, the juice is drawn off the skins and fermentation proceeds as with the production of white wines.

Sparkling Wines

All wines produce carbon dioxide as a by-product of fermentation. Sparkling wines manage, by various means, to capture this gas dissolved within the wine. This can be achieved by a variety of ingenious means. One prerequisite for the production of sparkling wines was the consistent creation of bottles strong enough to withstand considerable internal pressure without shattering. Early attempts to produce sparkling wines no doubt resulted in bottles exploding all over the place. But the outcome proved well worth the risk.

The classic and most laborious method of making sparkling wine is secondary fermentation in the bottle. This is used to produce some of the finest sparkling wines in the world, including champagne, franciacorta, cava and sparkling wines from elsewhere in the world, notably award-winning examples from England. Still base wines are first produced – in the case of champagne from a classic blend or cuvée of pinot noir, chardonnay and pinot meunier. The wines are bottled, then a secondary fermentation is provoked by adding additional yeast and sugar to the wine, and sealing the bottle (in early days, corks were tied down with string to stop them from being pushed out; today a crown cork is generally used). The yeast feeds on the sugar within the bottle, producing carbon dioxide, and this dissolves within the wine, making it effervescent.

However, if bubbles are one desired by-product of secondary fermentation, one undesired element is a yeasty sludge that is left behind – this must be removed in order to result in a finished sparkling wine that is crystal clear.

This stubborn sludge will not simply slide into the neck of the bottle. Rather, it must be nudged painstakingly over a period of days or weeks, either manually by giving a sharp twist to each individual bottle held in special racks or *pupitres*, or else by utilizing a machine that rotates a whole pallet of bottles, gradually moving the bottles from a near-horizontal position towards a more vertical one. Eventually the yeasty sludge is coaxed down each bottle until it comes to rest in a bottleneck now virtually upside down. To complete the process, the necks of the bottles are frozen, the crown corks are removed, the pressure within the wine ejects the frozen blocks of wine containing the yeast sludge and the bottles are then topped up with a dosage that lends a varying degree of sweetness to the finished wine. Finally the bottles are sealed with the finished corks, which are wired down to keep them in place, and a decorative capsule is placed over the neck of the bottle.

This classic method is expensive and labour intensive, but it does result in the sparkling wines with the most finesse, as well as the finest and most persistent bubbles. A considerably less expensive way of making sparkling wines is known as the *cuve close* method. The *cuve close*, 'closed tank', is just that: a large tank that can be sealed and kept under pressure. The secondary fermentation therefore occurs in the tank, not the bottle, and the carbon dioxide remains dissolved in the wine because the tank is sealed. Once the secondary fermentation is complete, the wines can be pumped from the tank under pressure directly to the bottling line. The yeasty sludge, meanwhile, remains at the bottom of the tank and is removed once the wine has been transferred. Such a method, it should be noted, is not only a means of producing sparkling wine more cost-effectively: sparkling wines made by the *cuve close* method (such as Italian prosecco from the classic heartland of Valdobbiadene-Conegliano north of Venice) are able to maintain a particularly attractive youthful freshness and vivacity.

Dessert Wines

The ingenuity of man in producing so many different styles and types of drink from a single agricultural product, the grape, never ceases to amaze. Consider, for a moment, the production of sweet dessert wines made from grapes affected by *Botrytis cinerea*, which shrivels them to near-raisin state, leaving them with an ugly mould on the surface. *Botrytis* only occurs under certain conditions, in certain microclimates, and not evenly every year. But affected grapes can produce the most glorious sweet dessert wines. The fungus concentrates the juice within the grapes and lends haunting, honeyed flavours and aromas that can be quite simply astonishing. Whether made from sémillon grapes grown in the Sauternes region near Bordeaux, chenin blanc grapes from the Loire Valley, riesling from Germany's Mosel or Rhine Valleys, or welschriesling from Austria's steamy Neusiedlersee, these wines undoubtedly rank among the greatest and most unique in the world.

An alternative ancient means of producing sweet wines dating back to the Greeks and even earlier, and which is still in use today, is to use semi-dried grapes. The process involves first harvesting fresh grapes, then leaving them out to dry either in the heat of the sun or laid out in well-ventilated sheds. The grapes shrivel, losing moisture in the process while concentrating grape sugars and intensifying flavours and aromas. Known as *passito*, these wines, like vin santo, zibibbo

Vin santo is a traditional dessert wine from Central Italy made from grapes that have been dried to a semi-raisin state. This concentrates grape sugars while intensifying flavour and aroma. The resulting wine, fermented in small sealed casks that suffer the heat of summer and the cold of winter, can be glorious and truly unique.

di pantelleria or recioto di soave, have ancient antecedents, connecting us directly with those that our ancestors may have enjoyed.

Fortified Wines

The struggle to produce consistently drinkable wine that is able to be conserved has long been the greatest challenge to winemakers. It is no coincidence, then, that wines historically considered the greatest in the world are those with the ability to be conserved for years and even decades: the wines of Bordeaux, Burgundy and the Rhône Valley, sweet wines from Sauternes, the Loire Valley and Germany, or Italian heavyweights such as brunello di montalcino, barolo and the like. Such great wines would generally have sufficient alcohol, tannin and acidity to enable them to be conserved for lengthy periods, and this would allow them to evolve and develop within the cask and bottle for decades – and sometimes much longer.

Another means of helping wines to stabilize, and thus become easier to conserve and transport, is fortification – that is, adding distilled alcohol to wine or to partially fermented grape must in order to make it more robust. Richly coloured and flavoured partially fermented wines from Portugal's Upper Douro, when fortified with brandy, could withstand long voyages by sea without deteriorating. Furthermore, these wines retained their residual sweetness and gained power, fire and a voluptuous texture and smoothness from the added spirits, and had the ability to age for upwards of decades in the bottle or cask. Such wines found particular favour in northern European countries where drinkers came to value and appreciate such rich and warming libations. Port is made in a huge variety of styles and types, from white port to vibrant young ruby port, wood-aged tawnies and, the pinnacle, vintage port from a single exceptional harvest only, bottled while still young and destined to age, mature and mellow for many decades.

Sherry is another historic fortified wine that was initially produced primarily for export markets in northern Europe and is now transported around the world. It is produced using a unique and ingenious system of fractional blending known as the *solera* system, whereby small quantities of wine are taken from the oldest casks which are then topped up with wines from the next oldest, and so on, right up to the youngest vintage. The system results in wines that can range from bone-dry, light in colour finos and manzanillas to amber dry or medium-dry amontillados; mahogany-coloured dry to very sweet oloroso and cream sherries; and finally to near-black, super sweet dessert examples made from sun-dried pedro ximénez grapes. In each case, a complex finished wine eventually emerges that has the character of older wines yet the freshness of the youngest.

Other historic fortified wines, developed mainly not for local consumption but for export markets, include marsala from western Sicily; málaga (known also as mountain); madeira, from the island off Africa; vermouth, a fortified wine that has also been aromatized with herbs, plants and other flavourings; and vins doux naturels from France, made from partially fermented muscat grapes fortified with grape brandy.

Vintages

Most, but not all, wines are the products of a single harvest only. There are exceptions. Non-vintage champagne is produced from wines from each year's harvest blended judiciously with old reserves to maintain a consistent house style. Most fortified wines (with the exception of vintage port) are blends from various years. In the case of sherry, the *solera* system ensures, for example, that wines from a 100-year-old *solera* will contain at least a tiny percentage of its oldest wines within the final blend.

Normally, however, bottles of table wine display on their labels the year or vintage in which the grapes were harvested. Naturally there may be considerable variation in climatic conditions – temperature, precipitation, hail (which can destroy vineyards), frost or rain at the time of flowering, or moisture laid down in the subsoil over the winter – from one year to the next. These factors can have a profound effect on both the quality and quantity of a vintage, resulting in real differences from one to the next.

In general, those vintages that are most prized result in grapes that have the optimum balance of sugar, acidity, tannin and other elements to allow for the production of wines with the potential to age and improve through maturation. Investors value such vintage years above all others because the resulting wines are likely to have the capacity not only to continue to improve in the bottle, but also to increase in monetary value.

However, it should be stressed that wines from such years should not necessarily be considered 'better' than wines from so-called lesser years which may nonetheless bring other pleasures. Indeed, wines from less-celebrated years are often ready to be enjoyed at a younger age than wines from the so-called great vintages; and they are often available at a cheaper cost, as an added bonus.

Each vintage is unique and should be judged as such. Vintage charts are available for various wine regions, though it should be noted that these give only the broadest guide. Variations will certainly exist within any given delimited vineyard area or region. Not only can climatic conditions vary even within small areas, but also, more importantly, human decisions taken throughout the course of a vineyard's year will have an equally significant effect on the style and quality of any estate's finished wines.

6
Final Thoughts

Of all of man's potable creations, wine is unique in its ability to uplift, nourish, inspire, heal, delight and intoxicate. Wine is so important that it is part of religious ritual; yet it is also considered a daily staple without which (for many) life might hardly seem worth living.

The future of wine seems secure, if not positively rosy. Wine is a product linked to the past, to generations of tradition, to the very *terroir* that gives it birth. Yet alongside tradition, innovation is a powerful and continual force in the evolution of wine. Indeed, in the coming years and decades, wine is likely to evolve more rapidly than ever before in its long and illustrious history.

Climate Change

Without doubt, climate change will have a dramatic effect on the world of wine. In fact, it is already having a dramatic effect. In established, quality wine-producing countries, average temperatures have increased. As a result grapes are often reaching very high levels of ripening, leading to wines that are higher in alcohol and lower in acidity, and which may

Pebblebed vineyard, Devon. One of the most exciting new wine regions for the production of sparkling wines is southern England. Could this be the result of climate change?

lack subtlety or aromatic complexity. On the other hand, due to warmer temperatures winegrowing areas that have previously only been marginal at best may find that climate change brings real benefits. As a result, new wine regions and countries may emerge in the future that are capable of producing quality wines.

Canada, with its cooler-climate vineyards, has been tipped as a country that may come to rival its neighbour to the south as a quality wine-producing country. Eastern European countries previously not associated with wine, such as Ukraine, Moldova, Croatia and Poland, may also emerge as serious quality producers in the decades to come. Meanwhile the UK, notably in existing and yet-to-be-planted vineyards across southern England and Wales, has the potential to be the source of quality white, rosé and even red table wines, as well as award-winning sparkling wines made by the classic method of secondary fermentation in the bottle. Indeed it is no surprise that champagne producers have already begun investing in vineyards in southern England that share similar soil to that found in the champagne vineyards of the Marne.

Climate change and global warming may bring benefits to some, but undoubtedly there will be losers too. Climate change and global warming may not just result in warmer temperatures. We are already seeing that these phenomena result in more extreme fluctuations in weather patterns, from excessive precipitation that can cause flooding to lengthy periods of drought. Some wine-producing countries and regions may suffer adversely from such climate changes, and simply become too hot and arid, or else too unseasonably wet or unpredictable, to allow for the large-scale cultivation of grapes throughout the year. At the moment, it is still too early to say for sure which weather patterns are likely to become established. What is no longer in doubt is that climate change is happening.

Technology

Ancient civilizations had sophisticated means of producing wine that depended on state-of-the-art technologies of their day. From intricate multi-level wine cellars to immense medieval wooden beam presses; from the creation of amphorae that could be stacked in the holds of Roman trading galleys, to the mastery of the creation of wooden, liquid-tight barrels and wine casks; from the use of leather *pellejos* and *botas* to the manufacture of glass bottles and natural corks: since the earliest days, the production of wine has gone hand in hand with developments in technology.

Over the past 150 years or so, scientific advances have led to a greater understanding of the scientific principles of winemaking. Louis Pasteur contributed greatly to an understanding of microbial activity during fermentation, and helped winemakers to have a greater measure of control during the winemaking process and to produce wines that were infinitely more stable than ever before.

In recent decades, the widescale introduction of temperature-controlled stainless-steel fermentation vessels has led to huge advancements in winemaking around the world. In the past, in many parts of the world, excessively hot temperatures at harvest time would result in wines that were coarse or baked in flavour and which often oxidized quickly. Today, stainless-steel fermentation vats can be sited in wine cellars or even outdoors in direct sunlight. A blanket of cold water around the tank ensures that the grape must (pressed from grapes often harvested early, even sometimes at night when temperatures are low) can be fermented at cool temperatures to result in fresh, clean styles of wine, even from grapes grown in hot areas, regions and countries.

There are so many advances in technology that have taken place over recent decades and which are continuing to come into mainstream production. Vineyards are now planted using sophisticated satellite imaging and lasers. Computers monitor every stage of production, in the vineyard as well as in the wine cellar. The use of complex technical processes such as micro-oxygenation to develop a more forward character in wines has become widely accepted. Oak character can be imparted through the use of oak staves inserted into stainless-steel vessels. There are myriad continuing advances in pest control and in dealing with maladies in the vineyard.

One area that could develop at a fast pace in coming years and decades, and which could conceivably have considerable impact on the production of wine in a short period of time, is the use of genetically modified technologies on both grape cultivars and yeasts. Natural selection has resulted in plant modifications that have occurred over centuries and even millennia. The genetic manipulation of DNA will allow such changes to be achieved in virtually no time at all.

Certainly, it is not difficult to envisage how genetic modification of grape cultivars could be of commercial benefit to industrial producers of wine. On a simple level, vines could be genetically modified to be more productive, to be more resistant to maladies and pathogens, or to grow with less need for pesticides or herbicides. If GM technology had been available at the end of the nineteenth century, would Europe's vineyards have had to be uprooted to eradicate *Phylloxera*?

The facility for manipulating crops is already in place and being used, so what is to stop such technology from being applied to the cultivation of *Vitis vinifera*? If GM tomatoes can be created that are blue or that have different flavour profiles, then similarly wine grapes could be genetically modified to have specific aromas or flavours, or to have more or less colour as well as greater yields or higher levels of fermentable sugar. These things may well be happening now. Furthermore there is ongoing research into the creation of genetically modified wine yeasts that may be quicker at initiating fermentation, more tolerant to sulphides, able to ferment at lower temperatures, or to work at higher alcohol levels. The commercial benefits to the wine producer, to be able to control such myriad variables, are potentially considerable.

Yet is such technology the way forward for wine? GM foods may or may not be harmful to health, but there is undoubtedly the potential for them to have a detrimental impact on both the environment and the global economy. Moreover, consumers have shown a marked collective resistance to their wholescale introduction.

More than this, there is a sense that wine has always been considered the most pure and natural of products. Moving its production from the vineyard and wine cellar into the scientist's laboratory may be, if not an outright dangerous step, then at least a commercially injudicious one. GM technologies may be capable of controlling some of the potentially problematic variables that arise with a natural product dependent on so many factors. While this could result in the industrial production of wines that are as consistent in flavour as manufactured soft drinks, the trade-off of course would be the loss of much of the individuality, the wonderful variety, the annual vagaries of vintages and indeed the very unpredictability that gives wine drinkers the most pleasure and surprise.

Packaging, Communications and Marketing

In the field of wine-bottle closure, natural cork is rapidly being replaced with artificial corks and with the Stelvin screw-cap. Not everyone applauds this change. For many, the aesthetic pleasure of drawing a natural cork is an integral part of the enjoyment of a bottle of wine. Furthermore, as the Stelvin system has now been in accepted use for quality wines for a period of years, there have been opportunities to compare the same wine in bottles sealed with both cork and screw-cap. Contrary to what proponents of Stelvin would have us believe, the latter does not always produce the best, freshest and cleanest results. Indeed, just as natural corks play their role in the evolution of a wine in the bottle, contributing to development of flavours and more complex bottle-aged bouquet, it appears that the screw-cap may have its own effect on the evolution of wine in the bottle. Indeed, some wine critics believe that the method of closure for a particular wine can be as important in determining character as the very provenance of the grapes themselves.

What about wine packaging? In a world where energy needs to be conserved, I wonder how long the glass bottle will continue to be the main form of packaging for wine? It is worth remembering that bottles have only been widely in use for around 300 years. Today the cost of transporting heavy wine bottles around the world is considerable and in many cases wines are already being shipped by sea in bladders within containers, to be bottled at the destination country. Why then even use a glass bottle? In 2011, the first paper wine bottle was launched. Weighing just 55 grams, compared with 500 grams for glass, the paper container looks like a bottle and is fully biodegradable. Though purists and wine snobs may turn their noses up at such a development, with landfill space at a premium, it seems certain that alternatives to glass may need to be found, and sooner rather than later.

Indeed, as bulk wines increasingly become manufactured products marketed as brands, and as a new generation comes to enjoy such alcoholic beverages without reference to the context of place or tradition that has long been associated with wine, then there will be no reason why other more imaginative forms of packaging will not be adapted, as has been the case with other heavily marketed drinks. My guess is that creative marketing trends may well increasingly seek to move a new generation of wine drinkers away from the traditional bottle and cork, which could come to be seen as incredibly old-fashioned.

If advanced scientific technology and changes to packaging are parts of a move towards wine becoming more of a manufactured, multinational, branded commodity, at the same time small individual producers will continue to fight their corner. One way they will do this will be by making the best use of global communication technologies to have a dialogue directly with their consumers. In the past, the only information that a wine producer could impart directly to a consumer was on the wine label itself. Today, wine producers' websites can include detailed information about methods of cultivation as well as technical production, plus tasting notes. Information on traditional food and wine can be included as well as videos that bring an interested consumer directly into the vineyard or cellar. Producers can communicate directly with the consumer by email, on electronic forums and by other means of digital communication.

Such information is no longer limited to the personal computer, either. Hand-held mobile devices and smartphones already have wine apps that connect producers directly with the consumer. A smartphone pointed at a QR barcode on a bottle in a wine shop can give the consumer a world of information. Some restaurants now offer diners wine lists on iPads, enabling consumers to click to find out more about a particular wine, thus offering the means to gain more information than the most knowledgeable sommelier could ever provide.

In an age where information is literally at our fingertips, there has never been a better opportunity for wine producers to communicate directly with those enjoying their wines. This is likely to accelerate in the future. Such direct communications are one powerful tool that will allow small artisan wine producers to compete against immense multinational conglomerates and brands.

A Return to Nature

Climate change may already be having an effect on the geography of the wine world. Technological and scientific developments and innovations relating to the cultivation of grapes and the production of wine may allow for more consistent and greater quantities of wine to be manufactured in countries all around the world. Genetic modification has the potential to assist winemakers in constructing wines to suit market needs and current tastes, but at what cost to our environment? Developments in packaging and the marketing of wines as global brands are trends that will continue. Already wines are being marketed varietally using an ever-decreasing number of popularly accepted international grape varieties at the expense of biodiversity. The end result is that wine is increasingly at risk of becoming a manufactured commodity rather than one with handcrafted individuality and personality.

Yet, at the same time, the longstanding traditions and culture of wine that have existed since almost the beginning

A return to the past: some producers today eschew the more uniform results that modern technology brings. In some cases they have returned to fermentation even in clay pots or amphorae, as our ancestors first did some thousands of years ago.

of time will, I am confident, remain. In contrast to the increasing power of the multinational brands, there is a realization among producer and consumer alike that small is often most beautiful. At historic wine estates where the same land has been worked literally for generations, as well as at new boutique properties started by enthusiasts whose aim is to make the best wines possible, there is a return to producing wines as they always have been in the past.

As more and more people are concerned about the purity and safety of what they choose to eat and drink, organic and bio-dynamic farming are increasingly viewed as significant and no longer niche pursuits. As a consequence there has been a considerable increase in the availability of organic and bio-dynamic wines. Knowing that the grapes used to produce a wine have been cultivated as naturally as possible and without excessive use of chemicals, additives or other sophistry is important to consumers and many are happy to pay the premium that such certified wines may command.

Even those producers who do not choose to have their wines certified by an official body may still aim to produce wines as naturally as possible. Indeed, alongside the rise in organic wines, there is a growing number of producers seeking to produce what are being called 'natural wines'. This means that the manufacturers may choose other methods of controlling pests and disease in the vineyards, such as using natural products, tissanes or sometimes introducing predator insects. In the cellar, natural yeasts present on the bloom of the grapes are taken advantage of, rather than being removed in favour of a cultured yeast supplied by a laboratory. For such natural wines, the use of sulphur both in the vineyard and in the winemaking processes is kept to a bare minimum or else eschewed altogether. Wines are stablized not by chemicals but by traditional methods such as simply moving the wine

Of all man's potable creations, wine has the unique capacity to bring pleasure to our lives. It is a celebratory libation, a comfort in times of sadness or sorrow, and simply an everyday beverage that makes us feel happy to be alive.

outside in winter to allow solids to precipitate naturally in the cold. Often such natural wines are not filtered, which means that they may present a sediment in the bottle. This is not seen as a defect but as a sign of goodness: to filter out natural elements present in the wine would be to lose something of the soul of the wine, say the proponents of such natural, and timeless, methods.

In the earliest days of the creation of wine, Neolithic producers fermented crushed grapes in rudimentary earthenware jars and pots; today some producers are choosing to return to such age-old methods, rejecting not only temperature-controlled stainless-steel but even wooden fermentation vessels, and instead fermenting in terracotta amphorae. The results are nothing less than fascinating.

Similarly, in a wine world that is seeing an ever decreasing number of grape varieties as the multinational conglomerates and big-brand wineries seek to find new ways to market their ubiquitous sauvignon blancs, chardonnays, shirazes, cabernets and merlots, there is at the same time a move to safeguard and indeed to celebrate obscure local and regional indigenous grape varieties. Such grapes may produce wines with flavours that are nothing like you have ever tasted before – a fact that is to be wholly applauded. The world is already awash with correct, clean, manufactured wines from a handful of international grape varieties grown and processed industrially, all around the world. There is a growing market for individual wines of real character and personality from indigenous and local grape varieties and hopefully this will increase in years to come.

The global history of wine is a long and fascinating story that is never-ending. It is a tale that takes us from the beginnings of civilization to the present day and beyond, and all around the world. It is a tale that should be savoured, glass of wine in hand, in all its glorious and infinite variety and colour. This little book is but a starting point in a voyage of discovery. I urge you to be intrepid, to be curious, to be adventurous – and above all to enjoy your wine intelligently, thoughtfully and joyously.

Recipes

Matching Food and Wine

Wine is a subject that seems to generate unnecessary mystique. One such area is the matching of the 'correct' wines and foods. The truth is, there should be no mystery to the matching of complementary comestibles. If you prefer to drink red wine with fish, then that is most definitely not a hanging offence. If your taste is for sweet white wine with a nice, rare, juicy steak, then that is what you should drink.

Taste is wholly personal and everyone has flavour combinations that they may prefer, come what may. Nonetheless, if you are interested in exploring the subject in greater depth, then giving considered thought and attention to the matching of food and wine can certainly add a delicious tier of enjoyment to a meal.

Regional combinations that have been tried and tested over the centuries and generations are generally successful. Sweet sauternes or monbazillac does really pair fantastically well with rich *foie gras de canard* or salty blue roquefort sheep's milk cheese, surprising though these combinations may sound. Other classic food and wine combinations may appear obvious. Asparagus is beautifully complemented by the pungent, grassy flavours of sauvignon blanc; shellfish tingle in your mouth when washed down with a sea-fresh wine rich in acidity such as muscadet or albariño; lamb cooked in a wood-fired oven is particularly mouth-watering when paired with the deep, rich, oaky flavours of a rioja reserva; bitter dark chocolate desserts, notoriously difficult to pair with wines, can be sublime when partnered by a raisiny, deeply sweet pedro ximénez sherry.

Often it is not the main element of a dish – sea bass, chicken, or venison – that dictates the choice of wine, but also all the various elements that go into the creation of a dish. These components need to be considered as well: are they sweet, acidic, herbal, for example? If so, then choosing a wine that complements these flavours is as important as matching it with the main component of the dish.

Naturally if you cook with wine, then the best wine to drink may be the same wine that has gone into the pot (unless you have cooked with 'plonk', which you most certainly should not do!). Classic dishes from the wine regions may trumpet the name of a wine, as in *coq au beaujolais*, *risotto al barbera*, *stracotto al chianti*. It would be near heresy to accompany such dishes with anything else (though there is nothing wrong with being a happy heretic).

Matching wine and food may be approached serendipitously ('What wine do we have in the house?') or it can be an altogether more considered science. If you are in a restaurant that has a sommelier, by all means take advantage of his or her expertise and ask for guidance based on what you are about to eat.

Just remember that after the theory, the strictures, the caveats, it really does all boil down to a question of personal taste. At the end of the day, drink what you like and be damned!

Wine is a perfect beverage on its own, with or without food. It can also be used as the base for some fabulous drinks. Here are three favourites.

Glühwein, aka *Vin Chaud* or Mulled Wine

Glühwein is the classic alpine winter drink. Hot spiced wine is perfect for warming yourself up from the inside out after a day of walking or skiing in the high mountains.

1 bottle full-bodied red wine (nothing too tannic or acidic)
1 stick cinnamon
6 cloves
2–3 tablespoons sugar (or to taste)
1 wine glass brandy
lemon or orange slices to decorate

Put the ingredients (except the lemon or orange slices) in a saucepan and bring to a bare simmer for about 10 minutes (do not boil or the alcohol will all evaporate). Serve in wine glasses or tumblers each decorated with a slice of lemon or lime.

Sangria

Sangria is a delightful drink. The virtual opposite of alpine *Glühwein*, it is the drink of Spain and Portugal, refreshing and invigorating in the heat of an Iberian summer.

1 bottle red Spanish or Portuguese wine
2 oranges, cut into slices
2 lemons, cut into slices
other seasonal fruit (strawberries, raspberries, etc)
sugar to taste
1 wine glass triple sec or brandy
200ml (7 fl. oz) lemonade or soda water

Mix all the ingredients and chill well. Sweeten to taste and serve in glasses over ice.

Spritz

This is the classic Venetian *aperitivo* to enjoy in typical *bacari* or bars throughout the watery city.

Campari or Aperol
Veneto white wine or sparkling prosecco
soda water
slices of lemon to decorate

Pour approximately 1 finger of Campari or Aperol into each glass, then top up with equal measures of Veneto white wine or sparkling prosecco and the same amount of soda water. Decorate with a slice of lemon.

Food with Wine Recipes

Forelle blaue or *truite au bleu* (blue trout)

For the classic 'blue trout' you need to ensure that the fish is extremely fresh and handled as little as possible. If you achieve this, then the fish does emerge a most striking and delicious shade of blue.

For the court bouillon
150 ml (5 fl. oz) white riesling or silvaner wine
4 tablespoons white wine vinegar
1 litre (36 fl. oz) water
1 carrot, sliced
1 onion, peeled and thinly sliced
1 bouquet garni
1 bay leaf

1 tablespoon salt
6 black peppercorns

For the trout
4 very fresh trout, gutted and cleaned but handled as little as
possible
freshly chopped parsley
slices of lemon

Put all the ingredients for the court bouillon into a large pan and
gently simmer for about 30 minutes. Place the trout in another
large pan and add enough court bouillon to just cover the fish.
Simmer for about 15 minutes (depending on the size of fish) or
until the fish turns blue and is fully cooked. Strain, arrange on a
platter and garnish with parsley and slices of lemon. Serve with
boiled potatoes.

Suggested wine: riesling kabinett from Mosel-Saar-Ruwer, silvaner
trocken from Franconia, or riesling d'alsace.

Mejillones al Jerez (mussels in sherry)

Steaming mussels in wine is a classic way of preparing this popular shellfish and many varieties of white wine may be used. Here
is the way it is done in Andalusia, using fino sherry.

1.5 kg (3 lb 5 oz) mussels, scraped and cleaned
glug of Spanish olive oil
2 whole garlic cloves, crushed
1 small onion, finely shopped
1 tablespoon flour
half-bottle fino sherry

Clean the mussels and discard any that do not shut when given a
sharp rap. Pour a glug of Spanish olive oil into a large, heavy-based
pot and gently sauté the garlic until soft. Add half the half-bottle

of fino to the pot and bring to a simmer. Add the scraped mussels and cook for about 5 minutes over a high heat until all the mussels have opened. Remove the mussels and set aside, reserving the cooking liquid.

Clean the pot, add a little more olive oil and gently sauté the chopped onions. Add the mussels' cooking liquid and the remaining sherry and bring to a simmer. Whisk in the flour to thicken the sauce and cook for a further 5 minutes or so. Return the mussels to the pot and coat well with the sauce. Serve with plenty of crusty bread to mop up the juices.

Suggested wine: fino sherry or manzanilla
Serves 2–4

Coq au vin

Stewing meat in wine has traditionally been a way of tenderizing old cuts and adding flavour. *Coq au vin* ought to be made with a cockerel, that is, an old boiling fowl, though younger birds are generally used these days. *Coq au vin* is the classic dish of Burgundy though other wine regions throughout the world have their own variations .

50 g (1¾ oz) butter
100 g (3½ oz) lardons or bacon cut into cubes
20 baby onions
1.5 kg (3 lb 5 oz) chicken, cut into 8 pieces
salt to taste
freshly ground black pepper
small glass of brandy
1 bottle young red wine (such as mâcon or beaujolais)
250 ml (9 fl. oz) rich chicken stock
1 bouquet garni
2 garlic cloves, peeled and crushed
2 bay leaves
sprig fresh thyme or marjoram
250 g (9 oz) button mushrooms

knob of butter mixed with flour (beurre manié)
freshly chopped parsley

Heat the butter in a large casserole and gently fry the lardons or bacon cubes. Add the baby onions and fry until golden. Remove and set aside. Add the seasoned chicken pieces and fry until browned. Return the onions and bacon to the pot. Heat the brandy in a ladle and set alight. Pour it flaming over the chicken and onions. Shake the pot backwards and forwards until the flames subside.

Add the red wine and sufficient stock to cover, along with the bouquet garni, crushed garlic, bay leaves and thyme or marjoram. Cook slowly for 45 minutes to an hour or until the chicken is just tender. Meanwhile, fry the button mushrooms whole to release their water, and add to the chicken and wine about 20 minutes before the end of the cooking time.

Remove the chicken, onions and mushrooms from the pan, place in a hot dish and keep warm in the oven. Skim off the fat from the cooking liquid, then raise the heat and boil rapidly to reduce. Remove the bay leaves and bouquet garni and correct the seasoning. Add the beurre manié to thicken the sauce to the consistency of double (heavy) cream. Pour the sauce over the chicken and serve at once, garnished with chopped parsley.

Suggested wine: mâcon rouge, beaujolais-villages, morgon, moulin-à-vent
Serves 4

Brasato al barolo (Beef Braised in Barolo)

Often the names of dishes grandly boast of the wines used in their cooking, as in *coq au chambertin* or in this case *brasato al barolo*. In our experience it is only when you dine in the house of a winemaker that you will truly experience such dishes – unless you make them yourself. Here is the way Elda Fontana of Cascina Fontana makes the classic dish of Le Langhe, using barolo drawn direct from the vat in the cellar below the kitchen.

1.5 kg topside of beef
1 bottle barolo
2 carrots, peeled and coarsely chopped
2 onions, peeled and coarsely chopped
2 sticks of celery, coarsely sliced
1 bay leaf
1 sprig rosemary
½ red pepper
2 garlic cloves, peeled and coarsely chopped
broth
glug of olive oil
knob of butter

Note: this dish is best prepared a day in advance.

In an earthenware, fireproof casserole or cast-iron pot, heat some olive oil and butter and brown the meat well. Add the chopped vegetables and cook until softened. Add about ½ litre of the barolo, cover the pot and continue to cook over a very low heat for about 90 minutes, checking from time to time and adding some stock or the remaining wine if the liquid is too reduced.

Once cooked, allow to cool, ideally overnight. The following day, take out the meat and cut into thick slices. Pass the vegetables through a food processor, return to the pan and reduce the liquid to the consistency of a thick sauce. Return the meat to the pot and heat through before serving.

Serve a slice of meat with some sauce spooned over. This is good accompanied by carrots, or by mashed potatoes and salad, or with polenta.

Suggested wine: barolo
Serves 4–6

Zabaglione alla marsala

Zabaglione is a delicious custardy dessert of whipped egg yolk, sugar and marsala wine. It is simple enough to make though it takes time and considerable effort to slowly and patiently whisk the mixture until it thickens. Marsala, the fortified dessert wine from western Sicily, is the classic wine used to make zabaglione, though you can experiment with other wines, such as moscato d'asti, for a lighter result.

6 egg yolks
6 tablespoons sugar
300 ml (10 fl. oz) marsala wine

Whisk together the egg yolks and sugar until creamy. Place in the top of a double boiler (or a pan that fits into another larger pan). Add water to the lower pan (ensuring that the water does not touch the base of the upper pan) and bring to a gentle simmer. While whisking the egg and sugar mixture continuously, gradually add the marsala. The water in the pan must not boil – if it did it could cause the egg to scramble. Keep whisking the mixture, incorporating the wine into the egg and sugar. It should increase in volume and become deliciously frothy as it heats up. When the mixture has thickened, spoon it into a glass or over a sponge cake and serve immediately.

Serves 4

Select Bibliography

Anderson, Burton, *Vino* (London, 1987)
—, *The Wine Atlas of Italy* (London, 1990)
Burk, Kathleen, and Michael Bywater, *Is This Bottle Corked?* (London, 2008)
Charters, Steven, *Wine and Society* (Oxford, 2008)
Clarke, Oz, *Let Me Tell you About Wine* (London, 2009)
—, *Wine Atlas* (London, 1995)
Johnson, Hugh, *The Story of Wine* (London, 2004)
—, *Wine Companion* (London, 2009)
—, and Robinson, Jancis, *The World Atlas of Wine* (London, 2007)
McGovern, Patrick E., *Ancient Wine: The Search for the Origins of Viticulture* (Princeton, NJ, 2003)
Millon, Marc, and Kim Millon, *The Wine and Food of Europe* (Exeter, 1982)
—, *The Wine Roads of France* (London, 1993)
—, *The Wine Roads of Italy* (London, 1991)
—, *The Wine Roads of Spain* (London, 1993)
Parker, Robert, *The Wine Buyer's Guide,* 7th edn (London, 2008)
Robinson, Jancis, ed., *The Oxford Companion to Wine* (Oxford, 2006)
—, *Vines, Grapes and Wines* (London, 1996)
Schuster, Michael, *Essential Winetasting* (London, 2009)
Smith, Barry, ed., *Questions of Taste: The Philosophy of Wine* (Oxford, 2007)
Stevenson, Tom, *The Sotheby's Wine Encyclopedia* (London, 2007)

Websites and Associations

Western and Eastern Europe

Austrian Wine
www.austrianwine.com

English Wine Producers
www.englishwineproducers.com

Wines of France
www.frenchwinesfood.com

Wines of Georgia
www.winesofgeorgia.com

Wines of Germany
www.germanwineusa.com

Greek Winemakers
www.greekwinemakers.com

Italian Made
www.italianmade.com

Wines of Portugal
www.winesofportugal.info

Wines from Spain
www.winesfromspainuk.com

North America

American Wine Society
www.americanwinesociety.org

California Winery Advisor
www.californiawineryadvisor.com

Wines of Canada
www.winesofcanada.com

South America

Wines of Argentina
www.winesofargentina.org

Wines of Chile
www.winesofchile.org

Australia, New Zealand and South Africa

National Wine Centre of Australia
www.wineaustralia.com.au

New Zealand Wine
www.nzwine.com

Wines of South Africa
www.wosa.co.za

Asia

China Wine Information
www.wines-info.com

Organizations

Alcohol in Moderation (AIM)
www.drinkingandyou.com

Institute of Masters of Wine
www.masters-of-wine.org

Sherry
www.sherry.org

Union des Grands Crus de Bordeaux
www.ugcb.net

Wine & Spirit Education Trust (WSET)
www.wset.co.uk

Wine Standards Board
www.wsb.org.uk

Acknowledgements

Learning about wine is a lifetime journey and I have been fortunate to have as my constant companion my wife Kim. Everything that I know about wine – the countless bottles tasted and enjoyed, the meetings with winemakers, the exploration of the wine lands, the discovery of stories within bottles – has been shared with her. Many of Kim's photographs illustrate this volume and she has also undertaken the meticulous picture research to source a range of illustrations that bring the story of wine vividly to life. I owe her an enormous debt (or at least a good bottle of barolo or two).

Andrew F. Smith, the Edible editor, has compiled a series that encompasses a fascinating range of subjects. I am grateful to him for inviting me to be a contributor and am proud to be a small part of it. I would like to thank Michael Leaman, publisher of Reaktion Books, for his understanding and patience while I took far longer to deliver this manuscript than anticipated. I would also like to thank Martha Jay and the Reaktion editorial and design teams for their care and vigilance in editing, proofing, and producing this book. In an age of electronic publishing where everything is done on-screen, with whole phases of production often overlooked, it is reassuring to find that the traditional publishing skills necessary for the careful editing and production of a book are still valued.

This small volume on an immense topic was from gestation to completion lubricated liberally and copiously by the sharing of wine and thoughts with many friends and companions. My brother David is a serious and knowledgeable wine connoisseur and we shared many bottles and discussions together, along with my sister Michele. I have on many occasions enjoyed discussing wine and literature, glass of something good in hand, with David Lynn, editor of the *Kenyon Review*. Winemakers Mario Fontana and Geoff Bowen are special friends; we have spent much time together sharing wines, learning, tasting, enjoying. Michael Caines, two-star Michelin chef, has probably the finest and most precise palate of anyone I've ever met: we have passed many enjoyable hours together tasting, discussing wine, food and the universe. Two special friends who have shared our most important life moments with us, most always over a glass of wine or two, are John and Jane Spree amongst other dear friends. Finally, it is a real pleasure for me that our children Guy and Bella have come to love wine as much as we do and that we can continue to taste, discover, learn, enjoy and travel together both overland to the wine country as well as through a wineglass.

Photo Acknowledgements

The author and the publishers wish to express their thanks to the below sources of illustrative material and/or permission to reproduce it:

Shutterstock: pp. 61, 62, 96–7, 98, 100–01, 104, 105, 108–9, 110, 113, 114, 116–17; British Museum Images: pp. 9, 10, 13, 14, 29, 30, 32, 33, 34, 39, 40, 42, 49, 51, 124; Kim Millon Photography: pp. 6, 16, 20, 24, 38, 44, 54, 58, 68, 74, 78, 79, 83, 88, 90, 125, 129, 131, 136, 142–3, 151, 152.

Index

italic numbers refer to illustrations; **bold** to recipes